Sir Patient Fancy

Aphra Behn

DODO PRESS

Sir Patient Fancy (1678)

Aphra Behn

Sir Patient Fancy

ACT I.

SCENE I.

A Roome.

Enter Lucretia with Isabella.

Isab.
'Tis much I owe to fortune, my dear *Lucretia*, for being so kind to make us Neighbours, where with ease we may continually exchange our Souls and thoughts without the attendance of a Coach, and those other little Formalities that make a business of a visit, it looks so like a Journey I hate it.

Lucr.
Attendance is that Curse to Greatness that confines the Soul, and spoils good Humour; we are free whilst thus alone, and can laugh at the abominable Fopperies of this Town.

Isab.
And lament the numberless impertinences wherewith they continually plague all young Women of Quality.

Lucr.
Yet these are the pretious things our grave Parents still chuse out to make us happy with, and all for a filthy Jointure, the undeniable argument for our slavery to Fools.

Isab.
Custom is unkind to our Sex, not to allow us free choice, but we above all Creatures must be forced to endure the formal recommendations of a Parent; and the more insupportable Addresses of an Odious Foppe, whilst the Obedient Daughter stands—thus—with her Hands pinn'd before her, a set look, few words, and a meine that cries—come marry me; out upon't.

Sir Patient Fancy

Lucr.
I perceive then what-ever your Father designes, you are resolv'd to love your own way.

Isab.
Thou maist lay thy Maiden-head upon't, and be sure of the misfortune to win.

Lucr.
My Brother *Lodwick*'s like to be a happy man then.

Isab.
Faith my dear *Lodwick* or no body in my heart, and I hope thou art as well resolv'd for thy Cozen *Leander*.

Lucr.
Here's my hand upon't I am, yet there's something sticks upon my Stomack, which you must know.

Isab.
Spare the Relation, for I have observ'd of late your Mother to have order'd her Eyes with some softness, her mouth endeavouring to sweeten it self into smiles and dimples, as if she meant to recall Fifteen again and give it all to *Leander*, for at him she throws her Darts.

Lucr.
Is't possible thou shou'dst have perceiv'd it already?

Isab.
Long since.

Lucr.
And, now I begin to love him, 'twou'd vex me to see my Mother Marry him,—well I shall never call him Father.

Isab.
He'l take care to give himself a better title.

Lucr.
This *Devonshire* Knight too who is recommended to my Mother as a fit Husband for me, I shall be so tormented with— My Brother swears he's the pertest unsufferable Fool he ever saw, when he was at my Uncles last Summer he made all his Diversion.

Isab.
Prethee let him make ours now, for of all Fops your Countrey Fop is the most tolerable Animal; those of the Town are the most unmanagable Beasts in Nature.

Lucr.
And are the most noysie, keeping Fops?

Isab.
Keeping begins to be as ridiculous as Matrimony, and is a greater imposition upon the liberty of man, the Insolence and Expence of their Mistresses has almost tir'd out all but the Old and Doting part of man-kind; The rest begin to know their value, and set a Price upon a good shape, a tolerable Face and Mein,—and some there are who have made excellent Bargains for themselves that way, and will flatter ye and gilt ye an Antiquated Lady as artfully as the most experienc'd Miss of 'em all.

Lucr.
Lord, Lord! what will this World come to—but this Mother of mine,—*Isabella.*

        [*Sighs.*

Isab.
Is discreet and vertuous enough, a little too affected, as being the most learned of her Sex.

Sir Patient Fancy

Lucr.
Methinks to be read in the Arts as they call 'em, is the peculiar Province of the other Sex.

Isab.
Indeed the men wou'd have us think so, and boast their Learning, and Languages, but if they can find any of our Sex fuller of words, and to so little purpose as some of their Gownmen, I'le be content to change my Petticoats for Pantiloons and go to a Grammar-school.

Lucr.
Oh they'r the greatest Babelards in Nature.

Isab.
They call us Easy, and Fond, and charge us with all weakness, but look into their Actions of Love, State, or War, their roughest business, and you shall find 'em sway'd by some who have the luck to find their feables; witness my Father, a man reasonable enough, till drawn away by doting Love and Religion: what a Monster my young Mother makes of him, Flatter'd him first into Matrimony, and now into what sort of Fool or Beast she pleases to make him.

Lucr.
I wonder she does not turn him to Christianity, methinks a Conventicle should ill agree with her humour.

Isab.
Oh she finds it the only way to secure her from his suspicion, which if she do not e're long give him cause for, I am mistaken in her Humour,—but see your

Enter L. Knowel and Leander.

Mother and my Cozen *Leander*, who seems, poor man, under some great Consternation, for he looks as gravely as a Lay-elder conducting his Spouse from a Sermon.

Sir Patient Fancy

La. Kno.
Oh fy upon't. See Mr. *Fancy* where your Cozen and my *Lucretia* are idling, *dii boni*, what an insupportable loss of time's this?

Lean.
Which might be better imploy'd if I might instruct 'em Madam.

La. Kno.
Aye Mr. *Fancy*, in Consultation with the Antients, —Oh the delight of Books! when I was of their age, I always imploy'd my looser hours in reading,—if serious, 'twas *Tacitus, Seneca, Plutarch's Morals*, or some such useful Author; if in an Humour gay, I was for Poetry, *Virgil, Homer*, or *Tasso*, Oh that Love between *Renaldo* and *Armida* Mr. *Fancy*! Ah the Caresses that fair *Corcereis* gave, and received from the young Warrier, ah how soft, Delicate and tender! upon my Honour I cannot read them in the Excellence of their Original Language, without I know not what Emotions.

Lean.
Methinks 'tis very well in our Mother tongue Madam.

La. K.
O Faugh Mr. *Fancy* what have you said, Mother tongue! Can any thing that's great or moving be exprest in filthy *English* ,—I'le give you an Energetical proof Mr. *Fancy*, observe but Divine *Homer* in the Grecian Language—*Ton d'apamibominus, Prosiphe, Podis Ochus Achilleus*! ah how it sounds! which English't dwindles into the most grating stuff:—then the swift Foot *Achilles* made reply,—oh faugh.

Lucr.
So now my Mother's in her right Sphere.

La. Kn.
Come Mr. *Fancy* we'le pursue our first design of retiring into my Cabinet and reading a leaf or two in *Martiall*, I am a little dull and wou'd fain laugh.

Lean.
Methinks Madam discourse were much better with these young Ladyes. *[Aside.* Dear *Lucretia* find some way to release me.

La. Kn.
Oh how I hate the impertinance of women, who for the generality have no other knowledge then that of dressing, I am uneasy with the unthinking Creatures.

Lucr. [Aside.
Indeed 'tis much better to be Entertaining a young Lover alone, but I'le prevent her if possible.

La. Kn.
No, I am for the substantiall pleasure of an Author. *Philosophemur*! is my Motto,—I'm strangely fond of you Mr. *Fancy*, for being a Scholar.

Lean.
Who Madam I a scholar? the greatest Dunce in Nature, —*[To them aside.* Malicious Creatures will you leave me to her mercy?

Lucr.
Prethee assist him in his misery, for I am Mudd, and can doe nothing towards it.

[Aside.

Isab.
Who my Cozen *Leander* a Scholar Madam?

Lucr.
Sure He's too much a Gentleman to be a Scholar.

Isab.
I Vow Madam he spells worse then a Country Farryer when he Prescribes a Drench.

Lean.
Then Madam I write the lewdest hand!

Isab.
Worse then a Politician or a States-man.

Lucr.
He cannot read it himself when he has done.

Lean.
Not a word on't Madam.

La. Kn.
This agreement to abuse him, I understand—

        [*Aside.*

—Well then Mr. *Fancy*, let's to my Cabinet—your hand.

Lean.
Now shall I be teas'd unmercifully,—I'le waite on you Madam.
        [*Exit Lady.*

—Find some means to redeem me or I shall be Mad.

        [*Exit. Lean.*
Enter Lodwick.

Lod.
Hah my dear *Isabella* here, and without a spy? what a blessed opportunity must I be forc't to lose, for there is just now arriv'd My

Sisters Lover, whom I am oblig'd to receive, but if you have a mind to laugh a little —

Isab.
Laugh! why are you turn'd Buffoon, Tumbler or Presbyterian Preacher.

Lod.
No, but there's a Creature below more ridiculous then either of these.

Lucr.
For loves sake what sort of Beast is that?

Lod.
Sir *Credulous Easie* your new Lover just come to Town Bag and Baggage, and I was going to acquaint my Mother with it.

Isab.
You'l find her well imploy'd with my Cozen *Leander*.

Lucr.
A happy opportunity to Free him, but what shall I doe now Brother!

Lod.
Oh let me alone to ruine him with my Mother, get you gon, I think I hear him coming, and this apartment is appointed for him.

Lucr.
Prethee haste then and free *Leander*, we'l into the Garden.

[Exeunt Lucr. and Isab.

A Chair and a Table.

Sir Patient Fancy

Enter Sir Credulous in a riding habit, Curry his Groom carrying a Portmantle.

Lod.
Yes—tis the Right Worshipfull, I'le to my Mother with the news.

[Exit Lod.

Sir Cred.
Come undoe my Portmantue and Equip me that I may look like somebody before I see the Ladies.—*Curry*, Thou shalt e'ne remove now *Curry* from Groom to Footman, for I'le ne're keep Horse more, no, nor Mare neither since my Poor *Gillian*'s departed this life.

Cur.
'Ds diggers, Sir, you have griev'd enough for your Mare in all conscience, think of your Mistress now Sir, and think of her no more.

Sir Cred.
Not think of her? I shall think of her whilst I live, poor Fool, that I shall, though I had forty Mistresses!

Curr.
Nay to say truth Sir, 'twas a good natur'd Civil beast, and so she remain'd to her last gasp, for she cou'd never have left this world in a better time, as the saying is, so near her journeys End.

Sir Cred.
A Civil Beast? Why was it Civilly done of her thinkest thou to dye at *Branford*, when had she liv'd till to morrow, she had been converted into Mony and have been in my Pocket? for now I am to Marry and live in town, I'le sell off all my Pads; poor Fool, I think she e'ne died for grief I wou'd have sold her.

Curr.
'Twas unlucky to refuse Parson *Cuffets* wifes money for her Sir.

Sir Cred.
Aye, and to refuse her another kindness too that shall be nameless which She offer'd me, and which wou'd have given me good luck in horse-flesh too, Zoz I was a modest fool that's truth on't.

Curr.
Well well Sir, her time was come you must think, and we are all Mortal as the saying is.

Sir Cred.
Well 'twas the lovingst titt,—but grass and hay she's gon—where be her shooes *Curry*?

Curr.
Here Sir, her Skin went for good Ale at *Branford*.

                  [gives him the shooes.

Sir Cred.
Ah! how often has she carry'd me upon these shooes to Mother *Jumbles*, thou remember'st her handsome Daughter and what pure Ale she brew'd, between one and t'other my Rent came short home there, but let that pass too, and hang sorrow as thou sayst, I have something else to think on.

            [Takes his things out, lays them upon the Table.

And *Curry*, as soon as I am drest, go you away to St. *Clements Church-yard*, to *Jackson* the Cobler there!

Curr.
What your Dog-tutor Sir?

Sir Cred.
Yes, and see how my whelp proves I put to him last Parlament.

Curr.
Yes Sir.
Enter Leander and starts back seeing Sir Cred.

Sir Cred.
And ask him what Gamesters come to the Ponds now adays, and what good Dogs.

Curr.
Yes Sir.

Lean.
This is the Beast *Lodwick* spoke of; how could I laugh were he design'd for any but *Lucretia*!

[Aside.

Sir Cred.
And dost hear, ask him if he have not sold his own Dog *Diver* with the white Ear, if I can purchase him, and my own Dog prove right, I'le be Duke of Ducking Pond ads zoz.

[*Sir Cred. dresses himself.*

Well, I think I shall be fine anon, he.

Curr.
But zo zo Sir, as the saying is, this Suit's a little out of fashion, 'twas made that very year I came to your Worship, which is five Winters and as many Summers.

Sir Cred.
What then Mun, I never wear it but when I go to be drunk and give my Voice for a Knight o'th'shire, and here at *London* in Term time, and that but Eight times in Eight Visits to Eight several Ladies to whom I was recommended.

Curr.
I wonder that amongst Eight you got not one Sir.

Sir Cred.
Eight! Zoz I have had Eight score Mun, but the Devil was in 'em, they were all so Forward, that before I cou'd seal and deliver, whip quoth *Jethro*, they were either all Married to some body else, or run quite away; so that I am resolv'd if this same *Lucretia* prove not right, I'le e'ne forswear this Town and all their false Wares, amongst which Zoz I believe they vent as many false Wives as any *Metropolitan* in Christendom, I'l say that for't and a Fiddle for't i'faith,—come give me my Watch out,—so, My Diamond Rings too, so, I think I shall appear pretty well all together *Curry* , hah?

Lean.
Like something Monstrously Ridiculous, I'l be sworn.

[*Aside.*

Curr.
Here's your Purse of broad Gold Sir, that your Grandmother gave you to go a wooing withall, I mean to show Sir.

Sir Cred.
Aye, for she charged me never to part with it,—so, now for the Ladyes.

[*Shakes his Ribbons.*

Lod.
Leander, what mak'st thou here, like Holy-day Fool gazing at a Monster?

[*Enter Lodwick.*

Lean.
Yes, and one I hope I have no great reason to fear.

Lod.
I am of thy opinion, away, my mother's coming, take this opportunity with my Sister, she's i'th' Garden, and let me alone with this Fool, for an Entertainment that shall shew him all at once, away—

[Exit Lean.

Lod. goes in to Sir Cred.

Sir Cred.
Lodwick, My dear Friend! and little spark of ingenuity!—Zoz man I'me but just come to Town.

[Imbrace.

Lod.
'Tis a joyful hearing Sir.

Sir Cre.
Not so joyful neither Sir, when you shall know Poor *Gillian* 's dead, My little gray Mare, thou knew'st her mun, Zoz 'thas made me as Melancholy as the Drone of a *Lancashire* Bagpipe, but let that pass, and now we talk of my Mare, Zoz I long to see this Sister of thine.

Lod.
She'l be with you presently Sir *Credulous*.

Sir Cre.
But hark ye, Zoz I have been so often fob'd off in these matters, that between you and I *Lodwick* if I thought I shou'd not have her, Zoz I'de ne'r lose precious time about her.

Lod.
Right Sir, and to say truth, these Women have so much Contradiction in 'em, that 'tis ten to one but a man fails in the Art of pleasing.

Sir Cre.
Why there's it,—therefore prethee dear *Lodwick* tell me a few of thy Sisters Humours, and if I fail,—then Hang me Ladies at your door, as the Song says.

Lod.
Why faith she has many odd Humours hard enough to hit.

Sir Cre.
Zoz let 'em be as hard as *Hercules* his Labours in the Vale of *Basse*, I'le not be frighted from attempting her.

Lod.
Why, She's one of those fantastick Creatures that must be courted her own way.

Sir Cre.
Why let's hear her way.

Lod.
She must be surpris'd with strange Extravagancies wholly out of the Road and Method of common Court-ship.

Sir Cre.
Shaw, is that all, Zoz I'm the best in Christendom at You're out of the way bus'nesses,—Now do I find the reason of all my ill success, for I us'd one and the same method to all I Courted, whatever their Humours were; Hark ye, prethee give me a hint or two, and let me alone to manage matters.

Lod.
I have just now thought of a way that cannot but take —

Sir Cre.
Zoz out with it man.
Lod.
Why, what if you should represent a Dumb Ambassador from the Blind God of Love.

Sir Cre.
How, a Dumb Ambassador? Zoz man how shall I deliver my Embassy then, and tell her how much I love her, —besides I had a pure speech or two ready by heart, and that will be quite lost.

        [Aside.

Lod.
Phy, phy! how dull you are! why; you shall do it by Signes, and I'le be your Interpreter.

Sir Cre.
Why faith this will be pure, I understand you now, Zoz I am old Excellent at Signes, —I vow this will be rare.

Lod.
It will not fail to do your bus'ness if well manag'd, — but stay, here's my Sister, on your life not a syllable.

        [Enter Lean. Lucr. and Isab.

Sir Cre.
I'le be rackt first, Mum budget,

        He falls back making Faces and Grimaces.

—prethee present me, I long to be at it, sure.

Lod.
Sister, I here present you with a worthy Knight, struck dumb with Admiration of your Beauty, but that's all one, he is employ'd Envoy extraordinary from the blind God of Love, and since like his young Master he must be defective in one of his Senses, he chose rather to be Dumb then Blind.

Lucr.
I hope the small Deity is in good health Sir?

Isab.
And his Mistress *Psyche* Sir?

He smiles and bows and makes Signes.

Lod.
He sayes that *Psyche* has been sick of late, but somewhat recovered, and has sent you for a

Looking every word upon Sir Credulous as he makes signes.

token a pair of Jet Bracelets, and a Cambrick Handkerchief of her own spinning, with a Sentence wrought in't; *Heart in hand, at thy Command.*

Sir Cred.
Zoz, *Lodwick* what do you mean? I'me the Son of an *Egyptian* if I understand thee.

Pulls him, he signes to him to hold his peace.

Lod.
Come Sir, the Tokens, produce, produce,—How! Faith I am sorry for that with all my heart,

He falls back, making damnable Signes. —he sayes—being somewhat put to't on his journey, he was forc't to

Pawn the Bracelets for half a Crown, and the handkerchief he gave his Landlady on the Road for a kindness received,—this 'tis when people will be fooling.—

Sir Cred.
Why, the Devil's in this *Lodwick*, for mistaking my Signes thus, hang me if ever I thought of Bracelets or a Handkerchief, or ever received a civility from any Woman breathing, —is he bewitch't trow?

[Aside.

Lean.
Lodwick, you are mistaken in the Knight's meaning all this while. Look on him Sir,—do not you guess from that look and wrying of his mouth, that you mistook the Bracelets for Diamond Rings, which he humbly begs, Madam, you would grace with your fair hand.

Lod.
Ah, now I perceive it plain.

Sir Creed.
A Pox of his Complement. Why this is worse than t'other,—What shall I do in this case?—should I speak and undeceive them, they would swear 'twere to save my Gems: and to part with 'em—Zoz, how simply should I look?—but hang't, when I have married her they are my own again.

[Gives the Rings and falls back into Grimaces.
Leander whispers to Lodwick.

Lod.
Enough,—Then Sister she has sent you a Purse of her own knitting, full of broad Gold,—

Sir Cre.
Broad Gold! why, what a pox does the Man Conjure?

Lod.
Which Sister faith you must accept of, you see by that Grimace how much 'twill grieve him else.

Sir Cre.
A pretty civil way this to Rob a man,—Why *Lodwick*—why what a Pox will they have no mercy,—Zoz I'le see how far they'l drive the jest.

[*Gives the Gold, and bowes and scrapes and screws.*

Lod.
Say you so Sir? Well I'le see what may be done,—Sister, behold him, and take pity on him, he has but one more humble request to make you, 'tis to receive a Gold Watch which he designs you from himself.

Sir Cre.
Why, how long has this fellow been a Conjurer? for he does deal with the Devil, that's certain,—*Lodwick,*—

[*Pulls him.*

Lod.
Aye do, speak and spoil all, do.

Sir Cred.
Speak and spoil all quoth he! and the Deuce take me if I am not provok't to't; why, how the Devil should he light slap dash, as they say, upon every thing thus? Well, Zoz, I am resolv'd to give it her, and shame her if she have any conscience in her.

[*Gives his Watch with pitiful Grimaces.*

Lod.
Now Sister you must know there's a mystery in this Watch, 'tis a kind of Hieroglyphick that will instruct you how a Married Woman of your Quality ought to live.

Sir Cred.
How, my Watch Mysteries and Hieroglyphicks! the Devil take me if I knew any such vertues it had.

[They are all looking on the Watch.

Lod.
Beginning at Eight, from which down to Twelve you ought to imploy in dressing, till Two at Dinner, till Five in Visits, till Seven at the Play, till Nine i'th' Park, at Ten at Supper with your Lover, if your Husband be at home, or keep his distance, which he's too well bred not to do, then from Ten to Twelve are the happy hours of the Bergere, those of intire enjoyment.—

Sir Cred.
Say you so? hang me if I shall not go near to think I may chance to be a Cuckold by the shift.

Isab.
Well Sir, what must she do from Twelve till Eight again?

Lod.
Oh those are the dull Conjugal hours for sleeping with her own Husband, and dreaming of Joys her absent Lover alone can give her.

Sir Cred.
Nay an she be for sleeping, Zoz, I am as good at that as she can be for her heart, or snoring either.

Lod.
But I have done; Sir *Credulous* has a dumb Oration to make you by way of farther Explanation.

Sir Cred.
A dumb Oration! Now do I know no more how to speak a dumb Speech than the Dog.

Lucr.
Oh I love that sort of Eloquence extreamly.

Lod.
I told you this would take her.

Sir Cred.
Nay, I know your silent Speeches are incomparable, and I have such a Speech in my head.—

Lod.
Your Postures, your Postures, begin Sir.

      He puts himself into a ready Posture as if he would speak, but onely makes faces.

Enter Page.

Pag.
Sir, My Lady desires to speak with you.

    [*To Lean.*

Lean.
I'le wait on her,—a Devil on't.—

Pag.
I have command to bring you Sir, instantly.

Lean.
This is ill luck Madam, I cannot see the Farce out, I'le wait on you as soon as my good fortune will permit me.

[Goes out.

Lucr.
He's going to my Mother, dear *Isabella* let's go and hinder their discourse: Farewel Sir Ambassador, pray remember us to *Psyche* , not forgetting the little Blind Archer, ha ha ha,—

[Ex. laughing.

Sir Cred.
So, I have undone all, they are both gone, flown I protest; Why what a Devil ail'd 'em? now have I been dumb all this while to no purpose, you too never told her my meaning right; as I hope to breath, had any but your self done this, I should have sworn by *Helicon* and all the rest of the Devils, you had had a design to have abus'd me, and cheated me of all my Movables too.

Lod.
What a hopefull project was here defeated by my mistake! but Courage Sir *Credulous*, I'le put you in a way shall fetch all about again.

Sir Cred.
Say you so? ah dear *Lodwick* let me hear it.

Lod.
Why, you shall this night give your Mistress a Serenade.

Sir Cred.
How! a Serenade!

Lod.
Yes, but it must be perform'd after an Extravagant manner, none of your dull Amorous night-walking noises so familiar in this Town, *Lucretia* loves nothing but what's great and Extravagant, and passes the reach of Vulgar practice.

Sir Cred.
What think you then of a silent Serenade? Zoz say but the word and it shall be done man, let me alone for Frolicks i'faith.

Lod.
A silent one? no that's to wear a good Humour to the stumps; I wou'd have this want for no noise, the Extreams of these two addresses will set off one another.

Sir Cred.
Say you so? what think you then of the Bagpipe, Tongs and Gridiron, Cat-calls and loud sounding Cymballs?

Lod.
Naught, naught, and of known use, you might as well treat her with Viols and Flute-doux, which were enough to disoblige her for ever.

Sir Cred.
Why, what think you then of the King of *Bantam*'s own Musick?

Lod.
How! the King of *Bantam*'s Musick!

Sir Cred.
Aye Sir, the King of *Bantam*'s: a Friend of mine had a Present sent him from thence, a most unheard of curiosity I'le assure you.

Lod.
That, that by all means Sir.

Sir Cred.
Well, I'll go borrow 'em presently.

Lod.
You must provide your self of a Song.

Sir Cred.
A Song! hang't 'tis but rummaging the Play-Books, stealing thence is Lawfull Prize—Well Sir *Cred*: your servant.

[Exit.

Enter Leander.

Lod.
I hope 'twill be ridiculous enough, and then the Devil's in't if it do not doe his Business with my Mother, for she hates all impertinent Noises but what she makes her self. She's now going to make a Visit to your Uncle, purposely to give me an opportunity to *Isabella*.

Lean.
And I'me ingag'd to wait on her thither, she designe to carry the Fiddles too, he's Mad enough already, but such a Visit will fit him for Bedlam.

Lod.
No matter, for you have all a lewd hand with him; between his continual imaginary sickness, and perpetual Physick, a man might take more Pleasure in an Hospital. What the Devil did he marry a young Wife for? and they say a handsome creature too.

Lean.
To keep up his Title of Cuckold I think, for she has beauty enough for temptation, and no doubt makes the right use on't: wou'd I cou'd know it, that I might prevent her cheating my Uncle longer to my undoing.

Sir Patient Fancy

Lod.
She'll be cunning enough for that, if she have wit: but now thou talk'st of intrigues, when didst see *Wittmore*? that Rogue has some lucky Haunt which we must find out.—But my Mother expects your attendance, I'le go seek my Sister, and make all the Interest there I can for you, whilst you pay me in the same Coin to *Isabella*.

[Adieu.

Lean.
Trust my Friendship—

[Exeunt severally.

The End of the First Act.

ACT II.

SCENE I.

A Garden.

Enter Lady Fancy, Wittmore and Maundy.

Witt.
Enough my Charming Mistriss, you've set my Soul at Peace, and chas'd away those Fears and Doubts my Jealousy created there.

Maun.
Mr. *Wittmore*'s satisfy'd of your constancy Madam, though had I been your Ladyship, I should have given him a more substantiall Proof, which you might yet doe, if you wou'd make handsom use of your time.

Witt.
Maundy advises well my Dearest, let's withdraw to yonder Covert Arbour, whose kind shades will secure us a happiness that Gods might envy.

[*Offers to lead her out.*

La. Fan.
I dare not for the world, Sir *Patient* is now asleep, and 'tis to those few Minutes we are oblig'd for this injoyment, which shou'd Love make us transgress, and he shou'd wake and surprize us, we were undone for ever; no let us imploy this little time we have in consulting how we may be often happy, and securely so: oh how I languish for the dear opportunity!

Witt.
And cou'd you guess what torments I have suffer'd in these few Fatal Months that have divided us, thou woud'st pity me.

La. Fan.
—but to our business; for though I am yet unsuspected by my Husband, I am eternally plagu'd with his company, he's so fond of me, he scarce gives me time to write to thee, he waits on me from room to room, hands me in the Garden, shoulders me in the Belcony, nay does the office of my women, dresses and undresses me, and does so smirk at his handy-work! in fine, dear *Wittmore*, I am impatient till I can have less of his company, and more of thine.

Witt.
Does he never goe out of Town?

La. Fan.
Never without me.

Witt.
Nor to Church?

La. Fan.
To a meeting-house you mean, and then too carries me, and is as vainly proud of me as of his Rebellious opinion, for his Religion means nothing but that, and Contradiction; which I seem to like too, since 'tis the best cloak I can put on to cheat him with.

Witt.
Right my fair Hypocrite.

La. Fan.
But dear *Wittmore*, there's nothing so Comicall as to hear me Cant, and even cheat those knaves the Preachers themselves that delude the Ignorant Rabble.

Witt.
What Miracles cannot your Eyes and Tongue perform!

La. Fan.
Judge what a fine life I lead the while, to be set up with an old Formal Doating sick Husband, and a Herd of snivelling grinning Hypocrites that call themselves the teaching Saints, who under pretence of securing me to the number of their Flock, do so sneer upon me, pat my Breasts and cry, fy, fy upon this fashion of tempting Nakedness.

> [through the nose.

Witt.
Dear Creature, how cou'd we laugh at thy new way of living, had we but some minutes allow'd us to injoy that pleasure alone.

La. Fan.
Think, dear *Wittmore* think, *Maundy* and I have, thought over all our devices to no purpose.

Witt.
Pox on't I'me the dullest Dog at Blotting, Thinking, in the world, I should have made a damnable Ill Town Poet; has he quite left off going to the Change?

La. Fan.
Oh, he's grown Cautiously rich, and will venture none of his substantiall stock in transitory Traffick.

Witt.
Has he no Mutinous Caball, nor Coffee-houses, where he goes religiously to consult the wellfare of the Nation?

La. Fan.
His imagin'd sickness has made this their Rendesvouz.

Witt.
When he goes to his blind Devotion, cannot you pretend to be sick? that may give us at least two or three opportunities to begin with.

La. Fan.
Oh! then I should be plagu'd with continual Physick and Extempore Prayer till I were sick indeed.

Witt.
Damn the Humorous Coxcombe and all his Family, what shall we do?

La. Fa.
Not all, for he has a Daughter that has good Humour, Wit, and Beauty enough to save her,—stay—that has jogg'd a thought as the learned say, which must jogg on, till the motion have produc't something worth my thinking.—

[Enter Roger running.

Maun.
Ad's me here's danger near, our Scout comes in such hast.

La. Fa.
Roger, what's the matter?

Rog.
My Master, Madam, is risen from sleep, and is come into the Garden,—See Madam he's here.

La. Fa.
What an unlucky, accident was this?

Witt.
What shall I do? 'tis too late to obscure my self.

La. Fa.
He see's you already through the Trees,—here— keep your distance, your Hat under your Arm, so, be very Ceremonious whil st I settle a demure Countenance.—

Maun.
Well, there never came good of Lovers that were given to too much talking; had you been silently kind all this while, you had been willing to have parted by this time.
Enter Sir Patient in a Night-gown, reading a Bill.

Sir Pat.
Hum,—Twelve Purges for this present *January*,— as I take it, good Mr. Doctor, I took but Ten in all *December*, —by this Rule I am sicker this Month than I was the last, —and good Master Apothecary methinks your Prizes are somewhat to high, at this rate no body wou'd be sick.—Here *Roger*, see it paid however,—Ha, hum.

[*Sees 'em and starts back.* What's here, my Lady Wife entertaining a lewd fellow of the Town? a flaunting Cap and Feather Blade?

La. Fa.
Sir *Patient* cannot now be spoken with. But Sir, that which I was going just now to say to you, was, that it would be very convenient in my opinion to make your addresses to *Isabella* ,—'twill give us opportunities. *[Aside]* We Ladies love no imposition, this is Counsel my Husband perhaps will not like, but I would have all Women chuse their Man, as I have done,—my dear *Wittmore*.

[*Aside.*

Sir Pat.
I profess ingenuously an excellent good Lady this of mine, tho' I do not like her Counsel to the young man, whom I perceive would be a suiter to my Daughter *Isabella*.

Wit.
Madam, should I follow my inclinations, I should pay my vows no where but there,—but I am inform'd Sir *Patient* is a man so positively resolv'd.—

La. Fa.
That you should love his Wife.

[*Aside.*

Wit.
And I'le comply with that resolve of his, and neither Love nor Marry *Isabella*, without his Permission, and I doubt not but I shall by my respects to him gain his consent,—to Cuckold him.

[*Aside.*

Sir Pat.
I profess ingenuously a very discreet young man.

Wit.
But Madam, when may I promise my self the satisfaction of coming again? For I'me impatient for the sight and enjoyment of the fair person I love.

La. Fa.
Sir, You may come at night, and something I will doe by that time shall certainly give you that access you wish for.

Wit.
May I depend upon that happiness?

La. Fa.
Oh, doubt not my power over Sir *Patient*.

Sir Patient Fancy

Sir Pat.
My Lady *Fancy*, you promise largely.

La. Fa.
Sir *Patient* here?

Wit.
A Devil on him, wou'd I were well off, now must I dissemble, profess, and lye most confoundedly.

Sir Pat.
Your Servant Sir, your Servant,—My Lady *Fancy*, your Ladiship is well entertain'd I see, have a care you make me not Jealous, my Lady *Fancy*.

La. Fa.
Indeed I have given you cause Sir *Patient*, for I have been entertaining a Lover, and one you must admit of too.

Sir Pat.
Say you so, my Lady *Fancy*?—Well Sir, I am a man of Reason, and if you shew me good causes why, can bid you welcom, for I do nothing without Reason and Precaution.

Wit.
Sir I have.—

Sir Pat.
I know what you wou'd say Sir, few words denoteth a wise head,—you wou'd say that you have an ambition to be my Son in Law.

Witt.
You guess most right Sir.

Sir Pat.
Nay Sir, I'le warrant I'le read a man as well as the best, I have studied it.

Witt.
Now Invention help me or never.

Sir Pat.
Your Name I pray?

Putting off his Hat gravely at every word.

Witt.
Fain-Love, Sir.

Sir Pat.
Good Mr. *Fain-Love,* your Countrey?

Witt.
Yorkshire, Sir.

Sir Pat.
What, not Mr. *Fain-Love*'s Son of *Yorkshire,* who was Knighted in the good days of the late Lord Protector?

[Off his Hat.

Witt.
The same Sir,—I am in, but how to come off again the Devil take me if I know.

Sir Pat.
He was a man of admirable Parts, believe me, a notable head-piece, a Publick-spirited Person, and a good Commonwealths man, that he was, on my word,—Your Estate Sir, I pray?

[*Hat off.*

Witt.
I have not impair'd it Sir, and I presume you know its value? For I'me a Dog if I doe.—

Sir Pat.
O' my word 'tis then considerable Sir, for he left but one Son, and Fourteen hundred Pounds *per annum*, as I take it, which Son I hear is lately come from *Geneva*, whither he was sent for vertuous Education. I am glad of your Arrival Sir,— Your Religion I pray?

Witt.
You cannot doubt my Principles, Sir, since educated at *Geneva* .

Sir Pat.
Your Father was a discreet Man, ah Mr. *Fain-love*, he and I have seen better dayes, and wish we cou'd have foreseen these that are arriv'd.

Witt.
That he might have turn'd honest in time, he means, before he had purchas'd Bishops Lands.

Sir Pat.
Sir, You have no Place, Office, Dependance or Attendance at Court I hope?

Witt.
None Sir.—Wou'd I had,—so you were hang'd.

La. Fa.
Nay Sir, you may believe, I knew his Capacities and Abilities before I would encourage his Addresses.

Sir Pat.
My Lady *Fancy*, you are a discreet Lady;—Well I'le marry her out of hand to prevent Mr. *Lodwick*'s hopes, for tho' the young man may deserve well, that mother of his I'le have nothing to do with, since she refused to marry my Nephew.

[*Aside.*

Enter Fany.

Fan.
Sir Father, here's my Lady *Knowell* and her Family come to see you.

Sir Pat.
How! her whole Family! I am come to keep open House; very fine, her whole Family! she's Plague enough to mortify any good Christian,—tell her, my Lady and I am gon forth; tell her any thing to keep her away.

Fan.
Shou'd I tell a lye Sir Father, and to a Lady of her Quality?

Sir Pat.
Her Quality and she are a Couple of impertinent things, which are very troublesome, and not to be indur'd I take it.

Fan.
Sir, we shou'd bear with things we do not love sometimes, 'tis a sort of trial Sir, a kind of mortification fit for a good Christian.

Sir Pat.
Why, what a notable talking Baggage is this! How came you by this Doctrine?

Fan.
I remember, Sir, you Preach'd it once to my Sister, when the old Alderman was the Text, whom you exhorted her to marry, but the wicked Creature made ill use on't.

Sir Pat.
Go your way for a Prating Huswife; go, and call your Sister hither. *[Exit Fanny.]*—Well I'me resolv'd to leave this Town, nay, and the World too, rather than be tormented thus.

La. Fa.
What's the matter Dear, thou dost so fret thy self?

Sir Pat.
The matter! my house, my house is besieged with impertinence, the intolerable Lady, Madam *Romance*, that walking Library of Profane Books is come to visit me.

La. Fa.
My Lady *Knowell*?

Sir Pat.
Yes, that Lady of eternal noise and hard words.

La. Fa.
Indeed 'tis with pain I am oblig'd to be civil to her, but I consider her Quality, her Husband was too an Alderman your friend, and a great Ay and no Man i'th' City, and a painful promoter of the good Cause.

Sir Pat.
But she's a Fop, my Lady *Fancy*, and ever was so; an idle conceited she Fop, and has vanity and tongue enough to debauch any Nation under Civil Government: but, Patience, thou art a vertue, and Affliction will come,—Ah I'me very sick, alas I have not long to dwell amongst the Wicked, Oh, oh. —*Roger*, is the Doctor come?
Enter Roger.

Rog.
No Sir, but he has sent you a small draught of a Pint, which you are to take and move upon't.

Sir Pat.
Ah,—Well I'le in and take it;—Ah—Sir, I crave your Patience for a moment, for I design you shall see my Daughter, I'le not make long work on't Sir, alas I would dispose of her before I die, Ah,—I'le bring her to you Sir, Ah, Ah.—

[Goes out with Roger.

La. Fa.
He's always thus when visited, to save charges,— But how dear *Wittmore* cam'st thou to think of a Name and Countrey so readily?

Witt.
Egad I was at the height of my invention, and the Alderman civilly and kindly assisted me with the rest; but how to undeceive him,—

La. Fa.
Take no care for that, in the mean time you'l be shrewdly hurt to have the way laid open to our enjoyment, and that by my Husbands procurement too: but take heed dear *Wittmore*, whilst you only design to feign a Courtship, you do it not in good earnest.

Witt.
Unkind Creature!

La. Fa.
I wou'd not have you indanger her heart neither: for thou hast Charmes will do't.—Prethee do not put on thy best looks, nor speak thy softest language; for if thou dost, thou canst not fail to undoe her.

VVitt.
Well my pretty Flatterer, to free her heart and thy suspicions, I'le make such aukward Love as shall perswade her, however she chance to like my Person, to think most lewdly of my parts,—But 'tis fit I take my leave, for if *Lodwick* or *Leander* see me here, all will be ruin'd, death I had forgot that.

La. Fa.
Leander's seldom at home, and you must time your Visits: but see Sir *Patient*'s return'd, and with him your new Mistress.
Enter Sir Patient and Isabella.

Sir Pat.
Here's my Daughter *Isabella*, Mr. *Fain-love*: she'l serve for a Wife, Sir, as times goe; but I hope you are none of those,—Sweet-heart—this Gentleman I have design'd you, he's rich and young, and I am old and sickly, and just going out of the world, and would gladly see thee in safe hands.

Maun.
He has been just going this twenty Years.

[*Aside.*

Sir Pat.
Therefore I command you to receive the tenders of his Affection.
Enter Fany.

Fan.
Sir Father, my Lady *Knowell*'s in the Garden.

La. Fa.
My Dear, we must go meet her in decency.

Sir Pat.
A hard case a man cannot be sick in quiet.—

[Goes out.

Isab.
A Husband, and that not *Lodwick*! Heaven forbid.

[Aside.

Witt.
Now Foppery assist to make me very ridiculous.— Death she's very pretty and inviting, what an insensible Dog shall I be counted to refuse the enjoyment of so fair, so new a Creature, and who is like to be thrown into my Arms too whether I will or not?—but Conscience and my vows to the fair Mother: No I will be honest,—Madam,—as Gad shall save me, I'me the Son of a Whore, if you are not the most Bell Person I ever saw, and if I be not damnably in love with you, but a pox take all tedious Courtship, I have a free-born and generous Spirit, and as I hate being confin'd to dull cringing, whining, flattering, and the Devil and all of Foppery, so when I give an heart I'me an Infidel, Madam, if I do not love to do't frankly and quickly, that thereby I may oblige the Beautiful receiver of my Vows, Protestations, Passions, and Inclination.

Isab.
You're wonderfull ingaging Sir, and I were an Ingrate not to facilitate a return for the Honour you are pleas'd to do me.

Witt.
Upon my Reputation, Madam, you're a civil well-bred Person, you have all the Agreemony of your Sex, *La Bell Talie, la Boon Mien, & reparteét bien*, and are *tout one toore*, as I'me a Gentleman, *fort agreeable.*—If this do not please your Lady, and Nauseate her, the Devil's in 'em both for unreasonable Women.—

[To Maund.

Fan.
Gemini Sister, does the Gentleman Conjure?

Isab.
I know not, but I'me sure I never saw a more affected Fop.

Maun.
Oh a damnable impertinent Fop, 'tis pity, for he's a proper Gentleman.

Witt.
Well if I do hold out, Egad I shall be the bravest young fellow in Christendome: but Madam, I must kiss your hand at present, I have some Visits to make, Devoirs to pay, necessities of Gallantry only, no Love ingagement by, *Jove* Madam, it is sufficient I have given my Parole to your Father to do him the honour of my Alliance; and an unnecessary Jealousie will but disoblige Madam your slave—Death these Rogues will see me and I'me undone.—

[*Exit.*
Enter Lady Fancy, Lady Knowell, Sir Credulous and Lucr. with other women and men.

La. Kno.
Isabella, your servant, Madam, being sensible of the insociable and solitary life you lead, I have brought my whole Family to wait on your Ladyship, and this my Son *in Futuro*, to kiss your hands, I beseech your Ladyship to know him son your humble servant: my Son and your Nephew Madam are coming, with the Musick too, we mean to pass the whole day with your Ladyship:—and see they are here.

Enter Lodwick pulling in Wittmore, Leander with them,

Lod.
Nay since we have met thee so luckily, you must back with us.

Witt.
You must excuse me Gentlemen.

Lod.
We'le show ye two or three fine women.

Witt.
Death these Rogues will ruine me—but I have business Gentlemen that—

Lean.
That must not hinder you from doing deeds of Charity, we are all come to teaze my Uncle, and you must assist at so good a work—come gad thou shalt make love to my Aunt,—I wou'd he wou'd effectually.

[*Aside.*

Lod.
Now I think on't, what the Devil dost thou make here?

Witt.
Here?—oh Sir—a—I have a design upon the Alderman.

Lod.
Upon his handsome Wife thou meanest? ah Rogue!

Witt.
Faith no,—a—'tis to—borrow Mony of him, and as I take it Gentlemen you are not fit persons for a man of Credit to be seen with, I pass for a graver man.

Lod.
Well Sir, take your Course—but egad he'le sooner lend thee his wife than his Money.

[Ex. Witt. they come in.

Lean.
Aunt I have taken the boldness to bring a Gentleman of my aquaintance to kiss your Ladiships hands.

Lod.
Thy Aunt!—death she's very handsom,—Madam your most humble servant.

[Kisses the La. Fan.

Lean.
Prethee imploy this Fool that I may have an opportunity to entertain thy Sister.

Lod.
Sir *Credulous*, what not a word? not a Complement? hah— be brisk man, be gay and witty, talk to the Ladies.

Sir Cred.
Talk to 'em? why what shall I say to 'em?

Lod.
Any thing so it be to little purpose.

Sir Cred.
Nay Sir, let me alone for that matter—but who are they prethee?

Lod.
Why that's my Lady *Fancy*, and that's her Daughter in Law, salute 'em Man.—

Sir Cred.
Fair Lady,—I do protest and vow, you are the most beautifull of all Mothers in Law, and the World cannot produce your equall.

Lod.
The Rogue has but one method for all Addresses.

[They laugh.

La. Kn.
Oh absurd! this Sir is the beautifull Mother in Law.

[To La. Fancy.

Sir Cred.
Most Noble Lady, I cry you mercy,

[Enter Sir Pat.

Then Madam as the Sun amongst the Stars, or rather as the Moon not in conjunction with the Sun but in her opposition, when one rises the other sets, or as the Vulgar call it Full moon—I say as the Moon is the most beautifull of all the sparkling lights, even so are you the most accomplisht Lady under the Moon— and Madam, I am extreamly sensible of your Charms and Celestial Graces.

[To Isabella.

Sir Pat.
Why this is abominable and insupportable.

Lucr.
I find Sir, you can talk to purpose when you begin once.

Sir Cred.
You are pleas'd to say so, Noble Lady; but I must needs say, I am not the worst bred Gentleman for a Country Gentleman that ever you saw, for you must know incomparable Lady that I was at the University three years, and there I learnt my Logick and Rhethorick, whereby I became excellent at Repartee, sweet Lady. As for my Estate, my Father dy'd since I came of Age, and left me a small younger Brothers Portion, dear Lady.

Lucr.
A younger Brothers Sir?

Sir Cred.
Ha ha, I know what you wou'd infer from that now; but you must know delicious Lady, that I am all the Children my Father had.

Lucr.
Witty I protest.

Sir Cred.
Nay Madam when I set on't I can be witty.

Lean.
Cruel *Lucretia* leave 'em, and let us snatch this opportunity to talk of our own affairs.

Sir Cred.
For you must know bright Lady, though I was pleas'd to rally my self, I have a pretty competent Estate of about 3000 l. a year, and am to marry Madam *Lucretia*.

La. Fan.
You're a happy man Sir.

Sir Cred.
Not so happy neither, inestimable Lady, for I lost the finest Mare yesterday—but let that pass, were you never in *Devonshire* Madam?

La. Fan.
Never Sir.

Sir Cred.
Introth and that's pitty sweet Lady, for if you lov'd Hawking, Drinking, and Whoring,—oh Lord, I mean Hunting, i'faith there be good fellows wou'd keep you company Madam.

Sir Pat.
This is a Plot upon me, a meer Plot.—My Lady *Fancy*, be tender of my reputation, Foppery's catching, and I had as lieve be a Cuckold as Husband to a vain Woman.

Sir Cred.
Zoz, and that may be as you say Noble Sir: Lady pray what Gentleman's this—Noble Sir, I am your most humble servant.

Sir Pat.
Oh cry you mercy Sir.

[*walks away.*

Sir Cred.
No offence dear Sir I protest, 'slife I believe 'tis the Master of the house, he look't with such authority—why who cares, let him look as big as the four Winds, East, West, North, and South, I care not this,—therefore, I Beg your Pardon Noble Sir.

Sir Pat.
Pray spare your Hat and Legs Sir, till you come to Court, they are thrown away i'th' City.

Sir Cred.
O Lord dear Sir, 'tis all one for that, I value not a Leg nor an Arm amongst Friends, I am a *Devonshire* Knight Sir all the world knows, a kind of Country Gentleman, as they say, and am come to Town to Marry my Lady *Knowells* Daughter.

Sir Pat.
I'm glad on't Sir.

> [*walks away, he follows.*

Sir Cred.
She's a deserving Lady Sir, if I have any Judgment, and I think I understand a Lady Sir in the right Honourable way of Matrimony.

Sir Pat.
Well Sir, that is to say you have been marryed before Sir, and what's all this to me good Sir?

Sir Cred.
Marryed before incomparable Sir! not so neither, for there's difference in men Sir.

Sir Pat.
Right, Sir, for some are Wits, and some are Fools!

Sir Cred.
As I hope to breath 'twas a saying of my Grandmothers, who us'd to tell me Sir, that bought Wit was best. I have brought money to Town for a small purchase of that kind, for Sir, I wou'd fain set up for a Country Wit—Pray Sir where live the Poets? for I wou'd fain be acquainted with some of them.

Sir Pat.
Sir I do not know, nor do I care for Wits and Poets. Oh this will kill me quite, I'l out of Town immediately.

Sir Cred.
But Sir, I mean your Fine railing Bully Wits, that have Vineger, Gall and Arsenick in 'em as well as Salt and Flame and Fire and the Devil and all.

Sir Pat.
Oh defend me! and what is all this to me Sir?

Sir Cred.
Oh Sir, they are the very Soul of Entertainment, and Sir, it is the prettiest sport to hear 'em rail and baule at one another—Zoz wou'd I were a Poet.

Sir Pat.
I wish you were, since you are so fond of being rail'd at—if I were able to beat him I would be much angry— but Patience is a Vertue, and I will into the Country.—

 [Aside.

Sir Cred.
'Tis all one case to me dear Sir,—but I should have the pleasure of railing again, *cum privilegio*, I love fighting with those pointless Weapons—Zoz Sir, you know if we men of quality fall out—(for you are a Knight I take it) why there comes a Challenge upon it, and ten to one some body or other is run through the Gills, why a pox on't I say this is very damnable, give me Poets Licence.—

La. Fa.
Take him off in pity.

 [To Leander.

Lod.
Indeed Railing is a Coin only currant among the Poets—Sir Credulous.—

Sir Pat.
Oh blest deliverance—what a profane wretch is here, and what a lewd world we live in—oh *London, London,* how thou aboundest in Iniquity, thy Young men are debaucht, thy Virgins defloured, and thy Matrons all turn'd Bawds! my Lady *Fancy,* this is not company for you I take it, let us fly from this vexation of spirit on the never-failing wings of discretion.—

        Going to lead Lady Fancy off—the Lady Knowell speaking to Isabella all this while.

La. Kn.
How! marry thee to such a Fop sayest thou? oh egregious!—as thou lovest *Lodwick* let him not know his name, it will be dangerous, let me alone to evade it.

Isab.
I know his fiery temper too well to trust him with the secret.

La. Kn.
Hark ye Sir, and do you intend to doe this horrible thing?—

Sir Pat.
What thing, my Lady *Knowell*?

La. Kn.
Why to marry your Daughter Sir.

Sir Pat.
Yes Madam.

La. Kn.
To a beastly town Fool? *Monstrum horrendum!*

Sir Patient Fancy

Sir Pat.
To any Fool, except a Fool of your Race, of your Generation.—

L. K.
How! a Fool of my Race, my Generation! I know thou meanest my son, thou contumelious Knight, who let me tell thee, shall marry thy Daughter *invito te*, that is, (to inform thy obtuse understanding) in spight of thee, yes shall marry her, though she inherits nothing but thy dull Enthusiasmes, which had she been legitimate she had been possest with.

Sir Pat.
Oh abominable! you had best say, she is none of my Daughter, and that I was a Cuckold.—

La. Kn.
If I should Sir, it would not amount to *Scandalum Magnatum* , I'le tell thee more; thy whole Pedigree,—And yet for all this *Lodwick* shall marry your Daughter, and yet I'le have none of your Nephew.—

Sir Pat.
Shall he so, my Lady *Knowell*? I shall go near to outtrick your Ladyship for all your Politick Learning. 'Tis past the Canonical hour as they call it, or I wou'd marry my Daughter instantly, I profess we ne're had good daies since these Canonicall Fopperies came up again, meer Popish tricks to give our Children time for disobedience,—the next Justice wou'd ha' serv'd turn, and have done the business at any hour, but Patience is a Vertue—*Roger*, go after Mr. *Fain-love*, and tell him I wou'd speak with him instantly.

La. Kn.
Come come Ladies, we lose fleeting time, upon my Honour we doe, for Madam as I said I have brought the Fiddles, and design to Sacrifice the intire Evening to your Ladyships Diversion.

Sir Cred.
Incomparable Lady, that was well thought on, Zoz, I long to be jigging.

Sir Pat.
Fiddles, Good Lord! why what am I come to! —Madam I take it, Sir *Patient Fancies* Lady is not a proper Person to make one at immodest Revellings, and Profane Masqueradings.

La. Fa.
Why? ah 'tis very true Sir, but we ought not to offend a Brother that is weak, and consequently a Sister.

Sir Pat.
An Excellent Lady this, but she may be corrupted, Ah she may fall, I will therefore without delay carry her from this wicked Town.

La. Kn.
Come come Gentlemen, let's in, Mr *Fancy* you must be my man—Sir *Credulous* come, and you sweet Sir, come Ladies, — *Nunc est saltandum,* &c.

[*Exeunt.*

Scene changes to a Chamber.

Enter Sir Patient as before, Lady Fancy, Wittmore, Maundy, and Roger with things.

Sir Pat.
Maundy fetch my Cloaths, I'll dress me and out of Town instantly— perswade me not. [*To Witt.*] *Roger*, is the Coach ready *Roger*?

Rog.
Yes Sir, with four horses.

Sir Patient Fancy

La. Fa.
Out of Town! oh I'm undone then, there will be no hopes of ever seeing *Wittmore*. [*Aside.*]—*Maundy* oh help me to contrive my stay, or I'm a dead Woman.—Sir, sure you cannot goe and leave your affairs in Town.

Sir Pat.
Affairs! what Affairs?

La. Fa.
Why your Daughter's Marriage Sir,—and—Sir,— not Sir but that I desire of all things in the World the blessing of being alone with you, far from the noise and lewd disorders of this filthy Town.

Sir Pat.
Most excellent Woman! ah thou art too good for sinfull Man, and I will therefore remove thee from the temptations of it—*Maundy*, my Cloaths—Mr. *Fain-love*, I will leave *Isabella* with my Lady *Fidget* my Sister, who shall to morrow see you married to prevent farther inconveniences.

La. Fa.
What shall I doe?

Maun.
Madam, I have a design, which considering his Spleen, must this time doe our business—'tis—[*Whispers.*]

La. Fa.
I like it well, about it instantly, hah—

[*Ex. Maundy.*

alas Sir,—what ails your Face? good Heav'n—look *Roger*.

Sir Pat.
My Face! why what ails my Face! hah!—

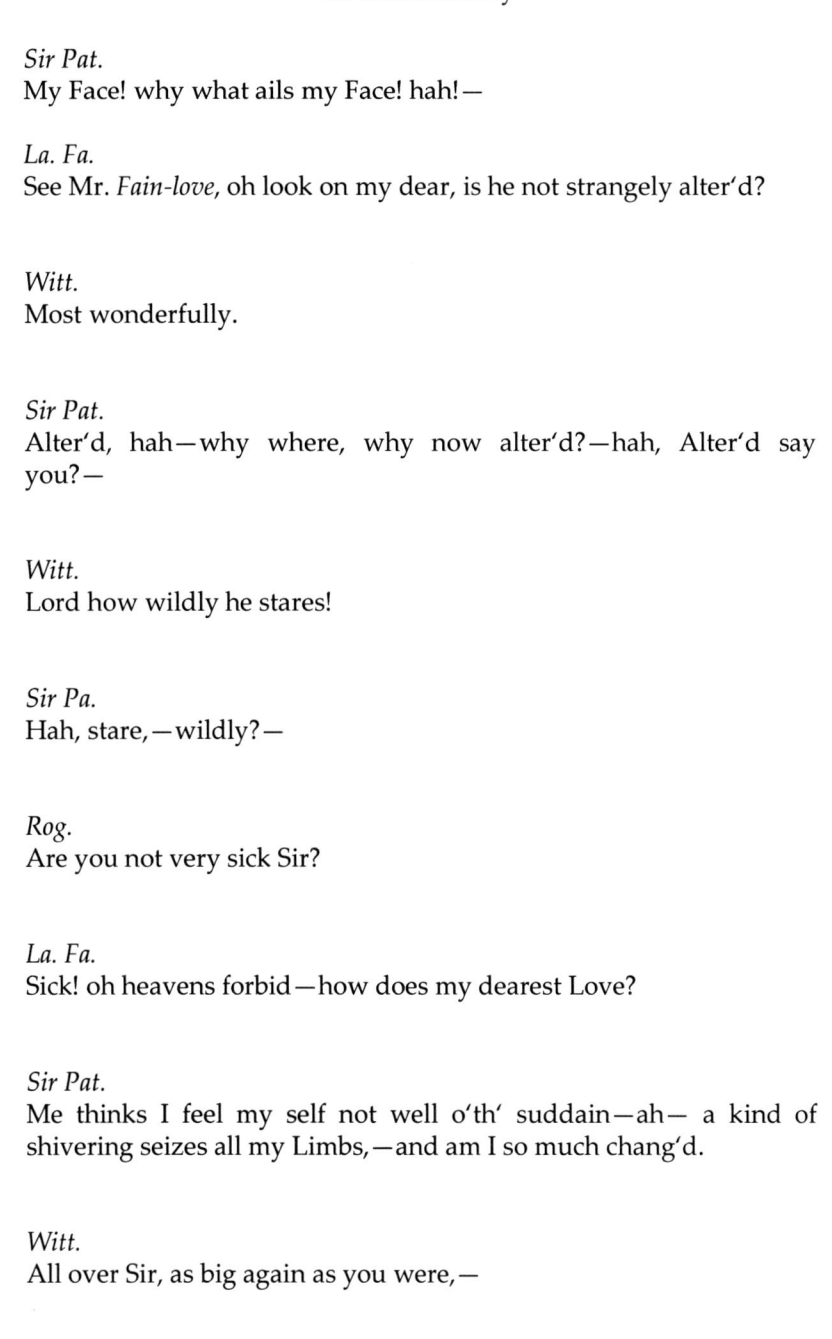

La. Fa.
See Mr. *Fain-love*, oh look on my dear, is he not strangely alter'd?

Witt.
Most wonderfully.

Sir Pat.
Alter'd, hah—why where, why now alter'd?—hah, Alter'd say you?—

Witt.
Lord how wildly he stares!

Sir Pa.
Hah, stare,—wildly?—

Rog.
Are you not very sick Sir?

La. Fa.
Sick! oh heavens forbid—how does my dearest Love?

Sir Pat.
Me thinks I feel my self not well o'th' suddain—ah— a kind of shivering seizes all my Limbs,—and am I so much chang'd.

Witt.
All over Sir, as big again as you were,—

Sir Patient Fancy

La. Fa.
Your Face is Frightfully blown up, and your dear Eyes just starting from your head, oh I shall sound with the apprehension on't.

[falls into Wittmore's Armes.

Sir Pat.
My head and Eyes so big say you,—oh I am wonderous sick o'th' suddain,—all over say you—oh oh—Ay I perceive it now, my Senses fail me too.

La. Fa.
How Sir, your Senses fail you?

Witt.
That's a very bad sign, believe me.

Sir Pat.
Oh Ay, for I can neither feel, nor see this mighty growth you speak off.

falls into a Chair with great signes of disorder.

Witt.
Alas I'm sorry for that Sir.

Rog.
Sure 'tis impossible, I'll run and fetch a Glass Sir.

[Offers to goe.

La. Fa.
Oh stay, I wou'd not for the world he should see what a Monster he is,—and is like to be before to Morrow.

[Aside.

Rog.
I'll sit him with a Glass—I'll warrant ye it shall advance our design.
Enter Maundy with the Cloaths, she starts.

Maun.
Good Heav'n what ailes you Sir?

Sir Pat.
Oh—oh—'tis so.

Maun.
Lord how he's swoln? see how his Stomach struts?

Sir Pat.
Ah 'tis true, though I perceive it not.

Maun.
Not perceive it Sir! put on your Cloaths and be convinc't—try'em Sir.

She pulls off his Gown and puts on his Doublet and Coat, which come not nearly a handfull or more.

Sir Pat.
Ah it needs not,—mercy upon me—

[falls back.

I'me lost, I'm gone, Oh man what art thou, but a Flower? I am Poyson'd, this talking Ladies breath's infectious; methought I felt the contagion steal into my heart; send for my Physicians and if I die, I'le swear She's my Murtherer, oh see see, how my trembling increases, oh hold my Limbs, I die.—
Enter Roger with a Magnifying Glass, shews him the Glass; he looks in it.

Rog.
I'le warrant I'le show his Face as big as a Bushel.

[Aside.

Sir Pat.
Oh, oh,—I'me a dead man, have me to bed, I die away, undress me instantly, send for my Physicians, I'me Poyson'd, my Bowels burn, I have within an *Ætna,*

They carry him out in a Chair.

My Brains run round, Nature within me reels.

Witt.
And all the drunken Universe does run on wheels.
ha ha ha.
Ah my dear Creature, how finely thou hast brought him to his journies end!

La. Fa.
There was no other way but this to have secur'd my happiness with thee, there needs no more then that you come anon to the Garden back-gate, where you shall find admittance,—Sir *Patient* is like to lie alone to night.

Witt.
Till then 'twill be a Thousand Ages.

La. Fa.

    At Games of Love Husbands to cheat is fair,
'Tis the Gallant we play with on the square.

        [Exeunt severally.

        The End of the Second Act.

Sir Patient Fancy

ACT III.

SCENE I.

Scene draws off and discovers Lady Knowell, Isabella, Lucretia, Lodwick, Leander, Wittmore, Sir Credulous, Other Men and Women, as going to Dance.

La. Kno.
Come one Dance more, and then I think we shall have sufficiently teaz'd the Alderman, and 'twill be time to part.—Sir *Credulous*, where's your Mistress?

Sir Cred.
Within a mile of an Oak, dear Madam, I'le warrant you,—well, I protest and vow, sweet Lady, you dance most Nobly,—Why, you Dance—like—like a—like a Hasty Pudding before *Jove*.

They Dance some Antick, or Rustick-Antick. Lodwick speaking to Isabella.

SONG Made by a Gent.

Sitting by yonder River Side
Parthenia thus to Cloe cry'd,
Whil'st from the fair Nymphs Eyes apace
Another Stream o'reflow'd her Beautious Face.
Ah happy Nymph, said she, that can
So little value that false Creature man.

Oft the perfidious things will cry,
Alass they burn, they bleed, they dye;
But if they're absent half a day,
Nay, let 'em be but one poor hour away,
No more they dye, no more complain,
But like unconstant wretches live again.

Lod.
Well, have you consider'd of that business yet *Isabella*?

Isab.
What business?

Lod.
Of giving me admittance to night.

Isab.
And may I trust your honesty?

Lod.
Oh doubt me not, my Mother's resolv'd it shall be a match between you and I, and that very consideration will secure thee, besides who wou'd first sully the Linnen they mean to put on?

Isab.
Away here's my Mother.
Enter Lady Fancy.

La. Fa.
Madam I beg your pardon for my absence, the effects of my Obedience, not Will; but Sir *Patient* is taken very Ill o'th' suddain, and I must humbly intreat your Ladiship to retire, for rest is onely essential to his recovery.

La. Kno.
Congruously spoken upon my Honour. Oh the impudence of this Fellow your Ladyships Husband, to espouse so fair a person only to make a Nurse of!

La. Fa.
Alas Madam!—

La. Kno.
A slave, a very houshold Drudg,—Oh faugh, come, never grieve,—for Madam, his Disease is nothing but imagination, a Melancholy which arises from the Liver, Spleen, and Membrane call'd *Mesenterium*, the *Arabians* name the distemper *Myrathial* , and we here in *England Hypochondriacal Melancholy*; I cou'd prescribe a most potent Remedy, but that I am loth to stir the envy of the College.

La. Fa.
Really Madam I believe,—

La. Kn.
But as you say Madam, we'l leave him to his repose, pray do not grieve too much.

Lod.
Death, wou'd I had the consoleing her, 'tis a charming Woman!

La. Kno.
Mr. *Fancy* your hand; Madam your most faithful Servant,— *Lucretia*, come *Lucretia*—your Servant Ladies and Gentlemen.—

La. Fa.
A Devil on her, wou'd the nimbleness of her Ladyships Tongue were in her Heels, she wou'd make more hast away, oh I long for the blest minute.—

Lod.
Isabella, shall I find admittance anon?

Isab.
On fair conditions.

Lod.
Trust my Generosity,—Madam your Slave.—

[Exit.

[To La. Fa. gazing on her, goes out.

Sir Cred.
Madam, I wou'd say something of your Charms and Celestial Graces, but that all praises are as far below you, as the Moon in her Opposition is below the Sun,—and so Luscious Lady, I am yours,—now for my Serenade,—

Exeunt all but La. Fa. and Maundy.

La. Fa.
Maundy, have you commanded all the Servants to Bed?

Maun.
Yes Madam, not a Mouse shall stir, and I have made ready the Chamber next the Garden for your Ladyship.

La. Fa.
Then there needs no more but that you wait for *Wittmore*'s coming to the Garden Gate, and take care no lights be in the House for fear of Eyes.

Maun.
Madam I understand Lovers are best by dark, and shall be diligent, the Doctor has secur'd Sir *Patient* by a sleeping Pill, and you are onely to expect your approaching happiness.

[Exeunt.

Sir Patient Fancy

SCENE II.
Lady Knowell's Chamber.

Enter Lady Knowell and Leander.

La. Kn.
Leander raise your Soul above that little trifle *Lucretia* ,—cannot you guess what better Fate attends you?— fie,—how dull you are!—must I instruct you in plain right-down termes?—and tell you—that I propose you Master of my fortune?—now possibly you understand me.
Enter Lucretia, and peeps.

Lean.

    I wish I did not Madam,
    Unless I'de vertue to deserve the Bounty;
    I have a Thousand faults Dissimulation hides,
    Inconstant, wild, debauch'd as youth can make me.

Lucr.
All that will not do your business.—
        [*Aside.*

La. Kn.
Yet you wou'd have my Daughter take you with all these faults, they're vertues there, but to the name of Mother, they all turn retrograde, I can endure a man

    As wild and as inconstant as she can,
    I have a Fortune too that can support that Humour,
    That of *Lucretia* does depend on me,
    And when I please is nothing;
    I'me far from Age or Wrinkles, can be Courted
    By Men as gay and youthful as a new Summer's morn,
    Beauteous as the first Blossoms of the Spring
    Before the common Sun has kiss'd their sweets away,
    If with salacious appetites I lov'd,

Lean.
Faith Madam I cou'd wish,—

La. Kn.

> That I were but Fifteen? but—
> If there be inequality in years,
> There is so too in Fortunes, that might add
> A Lustre to my Eyes, Charms to my Person,
> And make me fair as *Venus*, young as *Hebe*.

Lean.
Madam you have enough to ingage any unconquer'd heart, but 'twas, I thought, with your allowance I dispos'd of mine, and 'tis a heart that knows not how to change.

La. Kn.
Then 'tis a foolish unambitious heart, unworthy of the Elevation it has not Glorious Pride enough to aim at:— Farewell Sir,—when you are wiser, you may find admittance.

[Goes out.

Lean.
Stay Madam.—
Enter Lucretia.

Lucr.

> For what? to hear your Penitence? Forgive me Madam
> I will be a Villain, forget my vows of Love, made to
> *Lucretia* ,
> And Sacrifice both her, and those to interest.
> Oh how I hate this whining and dissembling!

Lean.
Do, Triumph o're a wretched man, *Lucretia*.

Lucr.
How! Wretched in loving me so intirely, or that you cannot marry my Mother, and be master of her mighty Fortune? 'Tis a temptation indeed, so between Love and Interest, hang me if ever I saw so simple a look as you put on when my Mother made Love to you.

Lean.
You may easily guess the confusion of a man in my circumstances, to be languishing for the lov'd Daughter, and pursu'd by the hated Mother, whom if I refuse will ruin all my hopes of thee.

Lucr.
Refuse her! I hope you have more wit?

Leand.
Lucretia, cou'd she make a Monarch of me, I cou'd not marry her.

Lucr.
And you wou'd be so wise to tell her so?

Lean.
I would no more abuse her, than I cou'd love her.

Lucr.
Yet that last must be done.

Lean.
How!

Lucr.
Dost believe me so wicked to think I mean in earnest? No, tell her me a fine story of Love, and liking, gaze on her, kiss her hands, and sigh, commend her face and shape, swear she's the miracle of the Age for wit, cry up her Learning, vow you were an Ass, not to be sensible of her perfections all this while, what a Coxcombe, to doat upon the Daughter when such charms were so visible in the Mother? Faith she'l believe all this.

Lean.
It may be so, but what will all this serve for?

Lucr.
To give us time and opportunity to deceive her, or I'me mistaken.

Lean.
I cannot teach my Tongue so much deceit.

Lucr.
You may be a fool and cry, Indeed forsooth I cannot love, for alas I have lost my heart, and am unworthy of your proffer'd blessings,—doe, and see her marry me in spight to this Fop *Easy* , this Knight of Nonsense; no, no, dissemble me handsomely and like a Gentleman, and then expect your good fortune.
Enter Antick.

Ant.
Madam, your Mother's coming.

Lucr.
Away then, she must not see us together, she thinks you gon.

Lean.
But must I carry off no comfort with me?

Lucr.
Will you expose me to the incens'd jealousy of a Parent? goe or I shall hate ye,—

[Thrusts him out.

SCENE III
SCENE *A Garden.*

Enter Maundy by dark: opens the Garden door.

Maun.
Now am I return'd to my old trade again, fetch and carry my Ladies Lovers, I was afraid when she had been married these night-works wou'd have ended, but to say truth, there's a Conscience to be used in all things, and there's no reason she shou'd languish with an old man when a young man may be had. —The door opens, he's come,—

[Enter Lodwick.

I see you're a punctual Lover Sir, Pray follow me as softly as you can.

Lod.
This is some one whom I perceive *Isabella* has made the Confident to our Amours.—

[Exeunt.

Scene draws off, and discovers La. Fancy in her Night-gown, in a Chamber as by the dark.

La. Fa.
Oh the agreeable confusion of a Lover high with expectation of the approaching bliss! What tremblings between joy and fear possess me? All my whole Soul is taken up with *Wittmore*, I've no Idea's, no thoughts but of *Wittmore*, and sure my tongue can speak no other language, but his name.— Who's there?
Enter Maundy leading Lodwick.

Sir Patient Fancy

Maun.
Madam, 'tis I, and your expected Lover here—I put him into your hands, and will wait your commands in the next Chamber.

[Ex. Maund.

Lod.
Where are you my dearest Creature?

La. Fa.
Here,—give me your hand, I'le lead you to those joys we both so long have sight for.

Lod.
Hah! to joys? sure she doth but dally with me,—

[Aside.

La. Fa.
Why come you not on my Dear?

Lod.
And yet, why this admission? and i'th' dark too, if she design'd me none but vertuous Favours?—What damn'd temptation's this?

La. Fa.
Are you bewitch'd, what is't that frights you?

Lod.

> I me fixt, Death, was ever such a Lover?
> Just ready for the highest joys of Love,
> And like a bashfull Girl restrain'd by fear
> Of an insuing Infamy,—I hate to Cuckold my own Expectations.

La. Fa.
Heavens! what can you mean?

Lod.
Death, what's this,—sure 'tis not Vertue in me,—Pray Heaven it be not impotence!—Where got I this damn'd honesty which I never found my self master of till now?—why shou'd it seize me when I had least need on't?

La. Fa.
What ails you? are you mad?—we are safe, and free as Winds let loose to ruffle all the Groves, what is't delays you then? Soft.

Lod.
Pox o' this thought of Wife, the very name destroys my appetite,

> Oh with what vigor I could deal my Love
> To some fair lewd, unknown,
> To whom I'de never made a serious vow?

La. Fa.
Tell me the Mystery of this sudden coldness? have I kept my Husband in Town for this? Nay, perswaded him to be very sick to serve our purpose, and am I thus rewarded!—ungrateful man!

Lod.
Hah,—'tis not *Isabella*'s voice,—your Husband say you?—

[Takes hold greedily of her hand.

La. Fa.

> Is safe, from any fear of interrupting us.
> Come—these delays do ill consist with Love
> And our desires; at least if they are equal.

Lod.

    Death 'tis the charming Mother!
    What lucky Star directed me to night!
    O my fair dear dissembler, let us haste
    To pay the mighty Tribute due to Love.

La. Fa.

    Follow me then with careful silence,—for *Isabella*'s
    Chamber joyns to this, and she may hear us.

Lod.

    Not Flowers grow, nor smooth streams glide away,
    Not absent Lovers sigh, nor breaks the day
    More silently than I'le those joys receive,
    Which Love and Darkness do conspire to give.
               [*Exeunt.*

Scene changes again to a Garden. Enter Isabella and Fanny in their Night-gowns.

Isab.
Well I have no mind to let this dear mad Devil *Lodwick* in to night.

Fan.
Why Sister, this is not the first venture you have made of this kind, at this hour, and in this place, these Arbours were they tell-tales, cou'd discover many pretty stories of your loves, and do you think they'l be less faithfull now? Pray trust 'em once again. Oh I do so love to hear Mr. *Lodwick* protest, and vow, and swear, and dissemble, and when you don't believe him, rail at you,—a vads 'tis the prettiest man—

Isab.
I have a strange apprehension of being surpris'd to night.

Fan.
I'le warant you, I'le sit on yon' Bank of Pinks, and when I hear a noise I'le come and tell you, so *Lodwick* may slip out at the back gate, and we may be walking up and down as if we meant no harm.

Isab.
You'l grow very expert in the arts of Love *Fanny*?

Fan.
When I am big enough I shall do my endeavour, for I have heard you say, Women were born to no other end than to love: And 'tis fit I should learn to live and die in my calling, —Come open the Gate or you'l repent it, we shall have my Father marry you within a day or two to that ugly man that speaks hard words.—a yads I can't abide him.

Isab.
What noise is that?

Fan.
Why 'tis Mr. *Lodwick* at the Garden door,—let him in whilst I'le to my Flowery Bank and stand Centinel.—

        [Runs off. Isabella opens the Gate.
Enter Wittmore.

Witt.
Who's there?

Isab.
Speak low, who should it be but the kind fool her self who can deny you nothing, but what you dare not take?

Witt.

> Not take! what's that? hast thou reserves in store?
> —Oh come and let me lead thee to thy Bed,
> Or seat thee on some Bank of softer Flowers,
> Where I may rifle all thy unknown store.

Isab.
How! surely you're not in earnest?—Do you love me?

Witt.

> Love thee! by thy dear self all that my Soul adores,
> I'me all impatient Flame! all over Love!
> —You do not use to doubt, but since you doe,
> Come, and I'le satisfy thy obliging fears,
> And give thee proofs how much my Soul is thine,
> I'le breath it all a-new into thy bosom,—
> Oh thou art fit for the transporting Play,
> All loose and wanton, like the Queen of Love
> When she descends to meet the Youth in shades.

Isab.
And are you Sir in earnest? can it be?

Witt.

> That question was severe, what means my Love!
> What pretty art is this to blow my flame,
> Are you not mine? did we not meet t'injoy?
> I came not with more vigorous eager hast,
> When our first Sacrifice to Love we paid,
> Than to perform that Ceremony now.
> Come do not let the Sacred Fire burn out
> Which only was prepar'd for Love's rich Altar,
> And this is the Divine, dark, silent Minute.—
>
> *[Goes to lead her off.*

Sir Patient Fancy

Isab.

Hold Ravisher, and know this sawcy Passion
Has render'd back your interest. Now I hate ye,
And my Obedience to my Father's will
Shall marry me to *Fain-love*, and I'le despise ye.

[Flings from him.

Witt.
Hah! *Isabella*! Death I have made sweet work,—stay gentle maid,—she'l ruin all if she goe—stay—she knew me, and cunningly drew me to this discovery; I'le after her and undeceive her.

[Runs after her.

A confus'd Noise of the Serenade, the Scene draws off to La. Fancy's Antichamber.

Enter Isabella groping as in the dark.

Isab.
Pray Heaven I get undiscover'd to my Chamber, where I'le make Vows against this perjur'd Man; hah, sure he follows still; no Wood Nymph ever fled before a Satyr, with half that trembling haste I flew from *Lodwick*,—oh he has lost his Vertue and undone me.

[Goes out groping, and the noise of Serenade again.

Scene changes to Lady Fancy's Bed-chamber, discovers her as before; Lodwick as just risen in disorder from the Bed: buttoning himself and setting himself in order; and noise at the door of unlatching it. Enter Isabella groping, Sir Patient without.

La. Fa.
It is this Door that open'd, and which I thought I had secur'd.

Sir Pat.
Oh insupportable, abominable, and not to be indur'd!

Isab.
Hah my Father! I'me discover'd and pursu'd,—grant me to find the Bed.

La. Fa.
Heav'ns 'twas my Husbands Voice, sure we're betray'd. It must be so, for what Devil but that of Jealousy, cou'd raise him at this late hour?

Isab.
Hah, where am I, and who is't that speaks.—

[*To her self.*

Lod.
So, he must know that I have made a Cuckold of him.

[*Aside.*

S. P.
Within, call up my men, the Coachman, Groom, and Butler; the Footmen, Cook and Gardener, bid 'em all rise and Arm, with long Staff, Spade and Pitchfork, and sally out upon the wicked.

Lod.
Short! what a death shall I dye,—is there no place of safety hereabouts—for there is no resisting these unmercifull Weapons.

Isab.
A mans Voice!

La. Fa.
I know of none, nor how to prevent your discovery.

Enter Sir Patient.

Sir Pat.
Oh oh lead me forward, I'le lye here on the Garden side, out of the hearing of this Hellish Noise.

La. Fa.
Hah Noise—what means he?

Lod.
Nay I know not, is there no escaping?—
Isab.
Who can they be that talk thus? sure I have mistook my chamber.

La. Fa.
Oh he's coming in—I'me ruin'd, what shall we doe? here—get into the Bed—and cover your self with the clothes— quickly—oh my Confusion will betray me.

> *Lodwick gets into the Bed, Isabella hides behind the Curtain very near to him.*

Enter Sir Patient led by Nurse and Maundy with Lights.

Maun.
Pray go back Sir, my poor Lady will be frighted out of her wits at this danger you put your self into, the noise shall be still'd.

La. Fa.
Oh what's the matter with my Love, what, do you mean to murder him? oh lead him instantly back to his Bed.

Sir Pat.
Oh oh, no, I'le lye here—put me to Bed, oh I faint, —my Chamber's possest with twenty thousand evil Spirits.

La. Fa.
Possest! what sickly Fancy's this?

Sir Patient Fancy

Sir Pat.
Ah the house is beset, surrounded and confounded with profane tinkling, with Popish Horn-Pipes and Jesuitical Cymballs, more Antichristian and Abominable then Organs, or Anthems.

Nurs.
Yea verily, and surely it is the spawn of Cathedrall Instruments plaid on by Babylonish Minstrells, only to disturb the Brethren.
Sir Pat.
Aye 'tis so, call up my Servants, and let them be first chastis'd and then hang'd, accuse 'em for French Papishes, that had a design to fire the City, or any thing—oh I shall dye— lead me gently to this Bed.

La. Fa.
To hinder him will discover all—stay Sir.—

Sir Pat.
Hah my Lady turn'd rebellious!

Throws himself forward to the Bed. —put me to Bed I say, hah—what's here— what art thou—a Man—hah, a Man, Treason! betray'd! my Bed's defil'd, my Lady Polluted, and I am Cornuted, oh thou Vile Serpent of my Bosome!

She stands with her Face towards the Stage in signes of fear.

Isab.
A Man, and in my Vertuous Lady Mothers Chamber! how fortunate was I to light on this discovery!

La. Fa.
Well, Sir,—since you have seen him, I beseech you for my sake, Dear, Pardon him this one time.

[Cokesing him.

Sir Pat.
Thou beg his Pardon? oh was ever heard such Impudence!

La. Fa.
Indeed my Love, he is to blame, but we that are judicious should bear with the frailties of Youth.

Sir Pat.
Oh insupportable Audacity!—what canst thou say false Woman?

La. Fa.
Truly not much in his defence my dear.

Isab.
Oh cunning Devil.—

La. Fa.
But Sir, to hide the weakness of your Daughter, I have a little strain'd my Modesty.—

Isab.
Heav'ns! what says she?—

La. Fa.
'Tis *Isabella's* Lover Sir, whom I've conceal'd.

Lod.
A good hint to save both our Credits.

Sir Pat.
How Mr. *Fain-love* mean you?

Sir Patient Fancy

Lodwick rises and comes a little more forward, Isabella does the like till both meet at the feet of the Bed and start, Lodwick looking simply.

La. Fa.
Aye my dear, Mr. *Fain-love.*

Lod.
Isabella here! must she know too what a fine inconstant Dog I am?—

Isab.
Lodwick! and in my Mothers Chamber! may I believe my Eyes?

Sir Pat.
But how got he hither—tell me that! oh Youth, Youth, to what degree of wickedness art thou arriv'd?

La. Fa.
She appointed him to come this night Sir, and he going to her Chamber, by mistake came into mine, it being the next to her's.

Maun.
But Lord Sir, had you heard how my Lady school'd him, whilst I ran down to fetch a light!

Lod.
Now does my Conscience tell me, I am a damn'd Villain.—

[*Aside, looking pitifully on Isabella.*

La. Fa.
But the poor Man presently perceiv'd his mistake, and beg'd my Pardon in such feeling termes—that I vow I had not the heart to deny it him.

Isab.
Oh Traytor! wou'd thou hadst been that Ravisher I took thee for, rather then such a Villain—false! and with my Mother too!

La. Fa.
And just then Sir you came to the door, and lest you shou'd see him, intreated me to hide him from your Anger, —the offence is not so hainous Sir, considering he's so soon to marry her.

Sir Pat.
—Well Sir, and what have you to say in your defence? —hah—how Mr. *Knowell!*—worse and worse—why how came you hither Sir? hah,—

La. Fa.
Not *Wittmore*! oh I am ruin'd and betray'd.

[falls almost in a sound.

Sir Pat.
Hah, *Isabella* here too!—

Isab.
Yes Sir, to justify her Innocence.—

Sir Pat.
Hah! Innocence! and justify! take her away, go out of my sight thou limb of Satan,—take her away I say, I'le talk with you to morrow, Lady fine tricks—I will.—

Isab.
—And I'le know before I sleep the mystery of all this, and who 'twas this faithless Man sent in his room to deceive me in the Garden.—

[Goes out.

Lod.
A plague of all ill-luck—how the Devil came she hither? I must follow and reconcile her.—

Going out, Sir Patient stays him.

Sir Pat.
Nay Sir, we must not part so till I have known the truth of this business I take it.

Lod.
Truth Sir, oh all that your fair Lady has said, Sir, I must confess, her Eyes have wounded me enough with Anger, you need not add more to my shame.—

La. Fa.
Some little comfort yet that he prov'd indeed to be *Isabella* 's Lover: oh that I should mistake so unluckily!

[Aside.

Sir Pat.
Why, I thought it had been Mr. *Fain-love.*

La. Fa.
By all that's good, and so did I.

Lod.
I know you did Madam or you had not been so kind to me: your servant dear Madam,—

Going, Sir Patient stays him.

La. Fa.
Pray Sir let him goe, oh how I abominate the sight of a man that cou'd be so wicked as he has been!

Sir Pat.
Ha,—good Lady, excellent woman, well Sir for my Ladies sake I'le let you pass with this, but if I catch you here again, I shall spoil your intrigues, Sir, marry-shall I, and so rest ye satisfy'd Sir.—

Lod.
At this time, I am Sir—Madam a thousand blessings on you for this goodness.—

La. Fa.
Ten thousand Curses upon thee,—go boast the ruine you have made.

[*Aside to Lod.*

Sir Pat.
Come, no more anger now my Lady; the Gentleman's sorry you see, I'le marry my pert Huswife to morrow for this, —*Maundy* see the Gentleman safe out,—ah—put me to Bed, ah—this nights work will kill me, ah, ah—

Ex. Lodwick and Maundy. The Scene draws over Sir Patient and Lady: draws again and discovers the Garden, Wittmore, Fanny and Isabella.

Isab.
How, Mr. *Fain-love*? it cannot be.—

Fan.
Indeed Sister 'tis the same for all he talks so, and he told me his coming was but to try your vertue only.
Enter Lodwick and Maundy as passing over, but stand.

Isab.
That *Fain-love* whom I am so soon to marry! and but this day courted me in another Dialect!

Witt.
That was my Policy Madam, to pass upon your Father with. But I'me a Man that knows the value of the Fair, and saw charms of Beauty and of wit in you, that taught me to know the way to your heart was to appear my self, which now I doe. Why did you leave me so unkindly but now?

Lod.
Hah, what's this? whilst I was grafting horns on another's head, some kind friend was doing that good office for me.

Maun.
Sure 'tis *Wittmore!* —oh that dissembler—this was his Plot upon my Lady, to gain time with *Isabella.*

        [*Aside.*

Witt.
And being so near my happiness, can you blame me, if I made a tryall whether your Virtue were agreable to your Beauty, great, and to be equally ador'd?

Lod.
Death, I've heard enough to forfeit all my patience— Draw Sir and make a tryall of your Courage too.—

Witt.
Hah! what desperate fool art thou?

        [*draws.*

Lod.
One that will see thee fairly damn'd e're yield his Interest up in *Isabella*—oh thou false Woman!

Sir Patient Fancy

[They fight out, Isabella and Maundy run off.

Scene changes to the long Street, a Pageant of an Elephant coming from the farther end with Sir Credulous on it, and several others playing on strange confused Instruments.

Sir Cred.
This sure is extraordinary, or the Devil's in't, and I'le ne're trust Serenade more.

[Come forward and all play again. —hold, hold, now for the Song, which because I wou'd have most Deliciously and Melodiously sung, I'le sing my self: look ye,—hum—hum.—

Sir Credulous should have Sung.

Thou grief of my heart, and thou Pearl of my Eyes,
D'on on Flannel Peticoat quickly, and rise:
And from thy resplendent window discover
A face that wou'd mortify any young Lover:
For I like great Jove Transformed do wooe,
And am Amorous Owl, To wit to woo, to wit to woo.

A Lover Ads Zoz is a sort of a tool
That of all things you best may compare to an Owl:
For in some dark shades he delights still to sit,
And all the night long he cries Wo to wit.
Then rise my bright Cloris and d'on on ship-shoe:
And hear thy Amorous Owl chant, Wit to woo, wit to woo.

—Well, this won't do, for I perceive no Window open, nor Lady-bright appear, to talk obligingly,—perhaps the Song does not please her, you Ballad-singers, have you no good Songs of another fashion?

1. Man.
Yes Sir, several, *Robin*,—Hark how the Waters fall, fall, fall,—

Sir Cred.
How Man! Zoz, remove us farther off, for fear of wetting.

1. Man.
No no, Sir, I only gave my fellow a hint of an excellent Ballad that begins—*I'll wodded joys how quickly do you fade.*

[*Sings.*

Sir Cred.
Aye, aye that, we'l have that,—*I'll wodded joys how quickly do you fade,*—[*Sings*] That's excellent! Oh now the Windows open, now, now show your capering tricks

[*Valting.*

[*They all play again. Enter a company of fellows as out of Sir Patient's House, led on by a precise Clerk, all armed with odd weapons.*

Abel.
Verily, verily, here be these Babes of Perdition, these Children of Iniquity.

Rog.
A pox of your Babes and Children, they are men and Sons of Whores whom we must bang confoundedly, for not letting honest godly People rest quietly in their Beds at Midnight.

Sir Cred.
Who's there?

Rog.
There with a Pox to you, cannot a Right-worshipful Knight that has been sick these Twenty Years with taking Physick, sleep quietly in his own House for you, and must we be rais'd out of our Beds to quiet your Hell-pipes in the Devil's name?

Abel.
Down with *Gog* and *Magog*, there, there's the rotten Bell-wether that leads the rest astray, and defiles the whole flock.

Rog.
Hang your Preaching and let's come to him, we'l maule him.

[Beat Sir Cred.

Sir Cred.
Oh Quarter Quarter, Murther, help, Murther, Murther.

Enter Lodwick.

Lod.
Damn these Rascalls who e're they were, that so unluckily redeem'd a Rival from my fury,—Hah, they are here,— Egad I'le have one touch more with 'em,—the dogs are spoiling my design'd Serenade too—have amongst ye,

Fights and beats 'em off.

—Sir *Credulous* how is't?

Sir Cred.
Who's there, *Lodwick*! Oh dear Lad, is't thou that hast redeem'd me from the inchanted Cudgels that demolish'd my triumphant Pageant, and confounded my Serenade? Zoz, I'me half kill'd man,—I have never a whole Bone about me sure.

Lod.
Come in with me—a plague upon the Rascal that escap't me.

[Exeunt.

The End of the Third Act.

ACT IV

SCENE I.

Lady Knowel's House.

Enter Lucretia followed by Sir Credulous.

Lucr.
Marry'd to morrow! and leave my Mother the possession of *Leander*? I'le die a thousand Deaths first,— How the Fool haunts me!

    [Aside.

Sir Cred.
Nay delicious Lady, you may say your Pleasure, but I will justify the Serenade to be as high a piece of Gallantry as was ever practised in our Age, tho' not comparable to your Charms and Celestial Graces, which shou'd I praise as I ought, 'twou'd require more time than the Sun employs in his Natural motion between the Tropicks; that is to say a whole Year, (for by the way, I am no *Copernican*) for, Dear Madam, you must know my Rhetorick Master,—I say my Rhetorick Master who was—

Lucr.
As great a Coxcombe as your self,—pray leave me I am serious,—I must go seek out *Lodwick*.

Sir Cred.
Leave ye! I thank you for that I'faith, before I have spoke out my speech, therefore I say Divine Lady—because my Rhetorick Master commanded the frequent use of *Hypallages, Allegories,* and the richest Figures of that beauteous Art,— because my Rhetorick,—

Lucr.
I must leave the Fool, follow if you dare, for I have no leasure to attend your nonsense.

[Goes out.

Enter Lady Knowell.

La. Kno.
What, alone Sir *Credulous*? I left you with *Lucretia*.

Sir Cred.
Lucretia! I'me sure she makes a very *Tarquinius Sextus* of me, and all about this Serenade,—I protest and vow, incomparable Lady, I had begun the sweetest Speech to her—tho' I say't, such Flowers of Rhetorick—'twou'd have been the very Nosegay of Eloquence, so it wou'd; and like an ungratefull illiterate Woman as she is, she left me in the very middle on't, so snuffy I'le warrant.

La. Kn.
Be not discourag'd Sir, I'le adapt her to a reconciliation, Lovers must sometimes expect these little *Belli-fugaces*, the *Grecians* therefore truly named Love *Glucupicros Eros*.

Sir Cred.
Nay bright Lady, I am as little discourag'd as another, but I'me sorry I gave so extraordinary a Serenade to so little purpose.

La. Kn.
Name it no more, 'twas onely a Gallantry mistaken, but I'le accelerate your felicity, and to morrow shall conclude the great dispute, since there is such Volubility and Vicissitude in Mundan affairs.—

[Goes out.

Enter Lodwick, stays Sir Credulous as he is going out the other way.

Lod.
Sir *Credulous*, whither away so fast?

Sir Cred.
Zoz, what a Question's there, dost not know I am to untie the Virgin Zone to morrow, that is, barter Maiden-heads with thy Sister, that is, to be Married to her man, and I must to *Lincolns-Inne* to my Counsel about it.

Lod.
My Sister just now told me of it, but Sir, you must not stir.

Sir Cred.
Why what's the matter?

Lod.
Have you made your Will?

Sir Cred.
My Will! no, why my Will man?

Lod.
Then for the good of your Friends and Posterity stir not from this place.

Sir Cred.
Good Lord, *Lodwick*, thou art the strangest Man, —what do ye mean to fright a body thus?

Lod.
You remember the Serenade last night?

Sir Cred.
Remember it! Zoz I think I do, here be the marks on't sure.—

Pulls off his Peruke and shews his head broke.

Lod.
Ads me, your head's broke.

Sir Cred.
My head broke! why 'twas a hundred to one but my neck had been broke.

Lod.
Faith not unlikely,—you know the next House is Sir *Patient Fancy's*; *Isabella* too you know is his Daughter.

Sir Cred.
Yes, yes she was by, when I made my dumb Oration.

Lod.
The same,—this Lady has a Lover, a mad, furious, fighting killing Hector, (as you know there are enough about this Town) this Monsieur supposing you to be a Rival, and that your Serenade was addrest to her—

Sir Cred.
Enough, I understand you, set those Rogues on to murder me.

Lod.
Wou'd 'twere no worse.

Sir Cred.
Worse! Zoz man, what the Devil can be worse?

Lod.
Why he has vow'd to kill you himself where-ever he meets you, and now waits below to that purpose.

Sir Cred.
Sha, sha, if that be all I'le to him immediately, and make *Affidavit* I never had any such design. Madam *Isabella*? ha, ha, alas poor man, I have some body else to think on.

Lod.
Affidavit! why he'l not believe you, should you swear your heart out, some body has possest him that you are a damn'd Fool, and a most egregious Coward, a fellow that to save your life, will swear any thing.

Sir Cred.
What cursed luck's this!—why how came he to know I liv'd here?

Lod.
I believe he might have it from *Leander* who is his friend.

Sir Cred.
Leander, I must confess I never lik'd that *Leander*, since yesterday.

Lod.
He has deceiv'd us all that's the truth on't, for I have lately found out too, that he's your Rival, and has a kind of a—

Sir Cred.
Smattering to my Mistress, hah, and therefore wou'd not be wanting to give me a lift out of this world, but I shall give him such a go-by—my Lady *Knowell* understands the difference between Three thousand a year and—prethee what's his Estate?

Lod.
Shaw—not sufficient to pay Surgeons Bills.

Sir Cred.
Alas poor Ratt, how does he live then?
Lod.
Hang him, the Ladies keep him, 'tis a good handsom fellow and has a pretty Town Wit.

Sir Cred.
He a Wit! what, I'le warrant he writes *Lampoons*, rails at Plays, curses all Poetry but his own, and mimicks the Players—ha,

Lod.
Some such common Notions he has that deceive the Ignorant Rabble, amongst whom he passes for a very smart Fellow, —'slife he's here.
Enter Leander.

Sir Cred.
Why—what shall I doe, he will not affront me before company? hah!

Lod.
Not in our house Sir,—bear up and take no notice on't.

[*Lod. whispers-Lean.*

Sir Cred.
No notice, quoth he? why my very fears will betray me.

Lean.
Let me alone,—*Lodwick*, I met just now with an *Italian* Merchant, who has made me such a Present!

Lod.
What is't prethee?

Lean.
A sort of specifick Poyson for all the Senses, especially for that of smelling, so that had I a Rival, and I shou'd see him at any reasonable distance, I cou'd direct a little of this Scent up to his Brain so subtlely, that it shall not fail of Execution in a day or two.

Sir Cred.
How—Poyson!

> *Shewing great signes of fear, and holding his Nose.*

Lean.
Nay should I see him in the midst of a thousand People, I can so direct it that it shall assault my Enemies Nostrils only, without any effects on the rest of the Company.

Sir Cred.
Oh—I'me a dead man!

Lod.
Is't possible?

Lean.
Perhaps some little sneezing or so, no harm; but my Enemy's a dead man Sir, kill'd.

Sir Cred.
Why, this is the most damnable *Italian* trick I ever heard of; why this out does the famous Poysoner Madam *Brenvilliers*, well, here's no jesting I perceive that, *Lodwick*.

Lod.
Fear nothing, I'le secure you.

> *[Aside to him.*

Enter Wittmore.—Wittmore! how is't friend! thou lookest cloudy.

Witt.
You'le hardly blame me Gentlemen, when you shall know what a Damn'd unfortunate Rascal I am.

Lod.
Prethee what's the matter?

Witt.
—Why I am to be Marry'd Gentlemen, Marry'd to Day.

Lod.
How, Marry'd! nay Gad then thou'st reason,—but to whom prethee?

Witt.
There's the Devil on't again, to a fine young, fair, brisk Woman that has all the temptations Heaven can give her.

Lod.
What pity 'tis they shou'd be bestow'd to so wicked an end! Is this your intrigue that has been so long conceal'd from your Friends?

Leand.
We thought 't had been some kind Amour, something of Love and Honour.

Lod.
Is she Rich? if she be wonderous Rich, we'le excuse thee.

Witt.
Her Fortune will be sutable to the Joynture I shall make her.

Lod.
Nay then 'tis like to prove a hopefull Match,—what a Pox can provoke thee to this, dost love her?

Witt.
No there's another Plague, I am cursedly in love elsewhere, and this was but a false address to hide that reall one.

Lod.
How, love another? in what quality, and manner?

Witt.
As a man ought to Love, with a good substantiall Passion, without any design but that of right-down honest Injoyment.

Lod.
Aye, now we understand thee, this is something! ah friend! I had such an adventure last night!—you may talk of you intrigues and substantiall Pleasures, but if any of you can match mine,—Egad I'le forswear womankind.

Lean.
An adventure! prethee where?

Sir Cred.
What, last night, when you rescu'd me from the Billbo-blades? indeed ye lookt a little furiously.

Lod.
I had reason, I was just then come out of a Garden from fighting with a man whom I found with my Mistress, and I had at least known who't had been but for the coming of those Rascalls that set on you, who parted us, whilst he made his escape in the crowd.

Witt.
Death! that was I, who for fear of being known got away, was't he then that I fought with, and whom I learnt lov'd *Isabella*!

[*Aside.*

Lod.
You must know Gentlemen, I have a sort of a Matrimoniall kindness for a very pretty woman, she whom I tell you I disturb'd in the Garden, and last night she made me an assignation in her Chamber: when I came to the garden Door by which I was to have admittance, I found a kind of Necessary call'd a Bawdy waiting-woman, whom I follow'd, and thought she wou'd have conducted me to the right woman; but I was luckily and in the dark led into a Ladies Chamber, who took me for a Lover she expected,—I found my happy mistake, and wou'd not undeceive her.

Witt.
This cou'd be none but *Lucia*.

[*Aside.*

—Well Sir, and what did you do there?

Lod.
Doe? why what dost think? all that a man inspir'd by Love cou'd doe, I followed all the Dictates of Nature, Youth and Vigor!

Witt.
Oh hold my heart—or I shall kill the Traytor.

[*Aside.*

Sir Cred.
Follow'd all the Dictates of Nature, Youth, and Vigour? prethee what's that?

Lod.
I kist a thousand times her balmy Lips, and greedily took in the nimble Sighs she breath'd into my Soul!

Witt.
Oh I can scarce contain my self.

[*Aside.*

Sir Cred.
Pshaw, is that all man?

Lod.

> I claspt her lovely Body in my Armes,
> and laid my Bosom to her panting Breast.
> Trembling she seem'd all love and soft desire,
> And I all burning in a youthfull fire.

Sir Cred.
Bless us, the Man's in a Rapture.

Witt.
Damnation on them both.

Sir Cred.
Well to the point man, what didst doe all this while.

Lean.
Faith I fancy he did not sleep, Sir *Credulous*.

Lod.
No friend, she had too many Charms to keep me waking.

Sir Cred.
Had she so? I shou'd have beg'd her Charms pardon, I tell her that though.

Witt.
Curse on my sloath, oh how shall I dissemble?

Aside.

Lean.
Thy adventure was pretty lucky—but *Wittmore* thou dost not relish it.

Witt.
My Minds upon my Marriage Sir,—if I thought he lov'd *Isabella* I wou'd marry her to be reveng'd on him, at least I le vex his Soul as he has tortur'd mine,—well Gentlemen, you'le dine with me,—and give me your opinion of my Wife.

Lod.
Where dost thou keep the Ceremony?

Witt.
At Sir *Patient Fancyes*, my Father in Law.

Lod.
How! Sir *Patient Fancy* to be your Father in Law?

Lean.
My Uncle?

Witt.
He's fir'd—'tis his Daughter Sir I am to Marry.—

Lod.
Isabella! Leander, can it be?—can she consent to this? and can she love you?

Witt.
Why Sir, what do you see in me, shou'd render me unfit to be belov'd?

[angry.

Lod.
Marry'd to day! by Heaven it must not be, Sir.

[draws him aside.

Witt.
Why Sir, I hope this is not the kind Lady who was so soft, so sweet, and charming last night.

Lod.
Hold Sir—we yet are friends.—

Witt.
And might have still been so, hadst thou not basely rob'd me of my Interest.

Lod.
Death! do you speak my Language?

[Ready to draw.

Witt.
No, take a secret from my angry heart, which all its friendship to thee cou'd not make me utter,—it was my Mistress you surpris'd last night.

Lod.
Hah, my Lady *Fancy* his Mistress? Curse on my prating Tongue.—

[Aside.

Sir Cred.
What a Devil's all this hard words, heart-burnings, resentments and all that?

Lean.
You are not quarrelling I hope, my friends?

Lod.
All this Sir we suspected, and smok't your borrowing Mony last night, and what I said was to gain the mighty secret that had been so long kept from your friends—but thou hast done a baseness.—

[*layes his hand on his Sword.*

Lean.
Hold, what's the matter?

Witt.
Did you not rob me of the Victory then I've been so long a toyling for?

Lod.
If I had 'twou'd not have made her guilty, nor me a Criminall, she taking me for one she lov'd, and I her for one that had no interest in my friend, and who the Devil wou'd have refus'd so fine a woman? nor had I, but that I was prevented by her Husband,—but *Isabella* Sir you must resign.

Witt.
I will, provided that our friendship's safe; I am this day to marry her, and if you can find a means to do't in my room, I shall resign my interest to my friend, for 'tis the lovely Mother I adore!

Sir Patient Fancy

Lod.
And was it you I fought with in the Garden?

Witt.
Yes, and thereby hangs a tale of a mistake almost equall to thine, which I'le at leasure tell you.

[Talks to Lod. and Lean.

Sir Cred.
I'me glad they're friends, Zoz here was like to have been a pretty business, what Damnable work this same womankind makes in a Nation of Fools that are Lovers!

Witt.
Look ye, I'me a Damn'd dull fellow at invention, I'le therefore leave you to contrive matters by your selves, whilst I'le go try how kind fortune will be to me this Morning, and see in what readiness my Bride is; what you do must be thought on suddainly, I'le wait on you anon, and let you know how matters goe,—I'me as impatient to know the truth of this, as for an opportunity to injoy *Lucia*.

[goes out.

Lod.
Leander what shall I doe?

Lean.
You were best—consult your Mother and Sister, women are best at intrigues of this kind: but what becomes of me?

Lod.
Let me alone to dispatch this fool, I long to have him out of the way, he begins to grow troublesome—but now my Mother expects you.—

Lean.
Prethee be carefull of me.—

[Ex. Leander.

Sir Cred.
What was this long whisper, something about me?

Lod.
Why yes faith I was perswading him to speak to his friend about this business, but he swears there's no hopes of a reconciliation, you are a dead man unless some cleanly conveyance of you be soon thought on.

Sir Cred.
Why, I'le keep within doors and defy malice and foul weather.

Lod.
O he means to get a warrant and search for stolen goods, prohibited Commodities or Conventicles, there's a thousand civill pretences in this Town to commit outrages—let me see.—

[They both pawse awhile.

Sir Cred.
Well I have thought,—and of such a business, that the Devil's in't if you don't say I am a man of intrigue.

Lod.
What is't?

Sir Cred.
Ha ha ha, I must have leave to laugh to think how neatly I shall defeat this son of a whore of a thunder thumping Hector.

Lod.
Be serious Sir, this is no laughing matter, if I might advise, you should steal into the Country, for two or three days till the business be blown over.

Sir Cred.
Lord, thou art so hasty and conceited of thy own invention, thou wilt not give a man leave to think in thy company, why these were my very thoughts, nay more, I have found a way to get off clever, though he watch me as narrowly as an inrag'd Serjeant upon an escape.

Lod.
That indeed wou'd be a Master-piece.

Sir Cred.
Why, look ye, do ye see that great Basket there?

Lod.
I doe,—this you mean.—

[*pulls in a Basket.*

Sir Cred.
Very well, put me into this Basket, and cord me down, send for a couple of Porters, hoist me away with a Direction, to an old Uncle of mine, one Sir *Anthony Bubleton* at *Bubleton-Hall* in *Essex*, and then Whip slap dash, as *Nokes* says in the Play, I'me gone and who's the wiser.

Sir Patient Fancy

Lod.
I like it well.

Sir Cred.
Nay lose no time in applauding, I'le in, the Carrier goes this morning, farewell *Lodwick*.—

[Goes into the Basket.

I'le be here again on Thursday.

[Lod. writes a direction.
Enter Boy.

Lod.
By all means Sir,—Who's there,—call a couple of Porters.

[Ex. Boy.

Sir Cred.
One word more, the Carrier lies at the Bell in *Friday-street*, pray take care they set me not on my head.—

[Pops in again.

Enter Boy and two Porters.

Lod.
Come hither, cord up this Basket, and carry it where he shall direct—*Leander* will never think he's free from a Rival till he have him in his possession,—To Mr. *Leander Fancy*'s at the next door; say 'tis things for him out of the Countrey.— Write a direction to him on the Basket lid.

[Aside to the Boy.

Porters going to carry off the Basket on a long Pole between 'em.

Enter Lady Knowel.

La. Kn.
What's this? whither goes this Basket?

Sir Cred.
Ah Lord! they are come with the Warrant.

[Peeps out of the Basket.

Lod.
Only Books Madam offer'd me to buy, but they do not please me.

La. Kn.
Books? nay then set down the Basket Fellows, and let me peruse 'em, who were the Authors, and what their Language?

Sir Cred.
A Pox of all Learning I say,—'tis my Mother-in-Law.

[Porters going to set down the Basket.

Lod.
Hold, hold Madam, they are only *English*, and some Law-*French*.

La. Kn.
Oh faugh, how I hate that vile sort of reading! up with 'em again fellows, and away.

The Porters take up and go out.

Lod.
God-a-mercy Law-*French*.

[*Aside.*

La. Kn.
Law-*French*! out upon't, I cou'd find in my heart to have the Porters bring it back, and have it burnt for a Heresy to Learning.

Lod.
Or thrown into the *Thames*, that it may float back to *Normandy* to have the Language new modell'd.

La. Kn.
You say well, but what's all this *ad Iphicli bonis*, where's Sir *Credulous* all this while? his affairs expect him.

Lod.
So does *Leander* your Ladiship within.

La. Kn.
Leander! Hymen, Hymenæe, I'le wait on him, *Lodwick* I am resolv'd you shall marry *Isabella* too, I have a design in my head that cannot fail to give you the possession of her within this two or three hours.

Lod.
Such an Indulgence will make me the happiest of men, and I have something to say to your Ladiship that will oblige you to hasten the design.—

La. Kn.
Come in and let me know it.

[*Exeunt.*

SCENE II.
A Table and Chairs.

Enter Lady Fancy in a Morning dress, Maundy with Pen, Ink, and Paper.

La. Fa.
Wittmore in the Garden saist thou with *Isabella*! Oh Perjur'd man it was by his contrivance then I was betray'd last night.

Maun.
I thought so too at first Madam, till going to conduct Mr. *Knowel* through the Garden, he finding Mr. *Wittmore* there with *Isabella*, drew on him, and they both fought out of the Garden, what mischief's done I know not,—but Madam, I hope Mr. *Knowel* was not uncivil to your Ladiship: I had no time to ask what past between you.

La. Fa.
Oh name it not! I gave him all I had reserved for *Wittmore*! I was so possest with the thoughts of that dear false one, I had no sense free to perceive the cheat,—but I will be reveng'd,—come let me end my Letter, we are safe from interruption.

Maun.
Yes Madam, Sir *Patient* is not yet up, the Doctors have been with him, and tell him he is not so bad as we perswaded him.

La. Fa.
—And was he soft and kind?—By all that's good she loves him, and they contriv'd this meeting,—my Pen and Ink—I am impatient to unload my Soul of this great weight of jealousie.—

[*Sits down and writes.*

Enter Sir Patient looking over her Shoulder a tip-toe.

Maun.
Heaven! here's Sir *Patient* Madam.

La. Fa.
Hah,—and tis too late to hide the Paper,—I was just going to subscribe my name.

Sir. Pat.
Good morrow, my Lady *Fancy*, your Ladiship is well imploy'd I see.

La. Fa.
Indeed I was, and pleasantly too, I am writing a Love-letter Sir,—but my Dear, what makes you so soon up?

Sir Pat.
A Love-letter!—let me see't.

[*Goes to take it.*

La. Fa.
I'le read it to you Sir.

Maun.
What mean you Madam?

[*Aside.*

Lady Fancy Reads.
It was but yesterday you swore you lov'd me, and I poor easy fool believed, but your last nights Infidelity has undeceived my heart, and rendred you the falsest Man that ever Woman sight for. Tell me, how durst you, when I had prepared all things for our enjoyment, be so great a Devil to deceive my languishing expectations? And in your room send one that has undone—
Your —

Maun.
Sure she's mad to read this to him.

Sir Pat.
Hum,—I profess ingenuously—I think it is indeed a Love-letter,—my Lady *Fancy* what means all this? as I take it here are Riddles and Mysteries in this business.

La. Fa.
Which thus Sir I'le unfold.—

Takes the Pen and writes Isabella.

Sir Pat.
How! undone—your—*Isabella*, meaning my Daughter?

La. Fa.
Yes my Dear, going this morning into her Chamber, she not being there, I took up a Letter that lay open on her Table, and out of curiosity read it, as near as I can remember 'twas to this purpose, I writ it out now because I had a mind thou shou'd'st see't; for I can hide nothing from thee.

Sir Pat.
A very good Lady I profess, to whom is it directed?

La. Fa.
Why,—Sir,—What shall I say, I cannot lay it now on *Lodwick* .—
                    [*Aside.*
I believe she meant it to Mr. *Fain-love*, for whom else cou'd it be design'd? she being so soon to marry him.

Sir Pat.
Hah,—Mr. *Fain-love*! so soon so fond and amorous!

La. Fa.
Alas, 'tis the excusable fault of all young Women, thou knowest I was just such another fool to thee, so fond— and so in love.—

Sir Pat.
Ha,—thou wert indeed my Lady *Fancy*, indeed thou wert,—but I will keep the Letter however, that this idle Baggage may know I understand her tricks and intrigues.—

[Puts up the Letter.

La. Fa.
Nay then 'twill out: no I beseech you Sir give me the Letter, I wou'd not for the World *Isabella* shou'd know of my theft, 'twou'd appear malicious in me,—besides Sir, it does not befit your Gravity to be concern'd in the little quarrels of Lovers.

Sir Pat.
Lovers! Tell me not of Lovers, my Lady *Fancy*; with Reverence to your good Ladiship, I value not whether there be love between 'em or not, Pious Wedlock is my business, —nay, I will let him know his own too, that I will, with your Ladiship's permission.

La. Fa.
How unlucky I am!—Sir, as to his Chastisement, use your own discretion, in which you do abound most plentifully, —but pray let not *Isabella* hear of it, for as I wou'd preserve my duty to thee, by communicating all things to thee, so I wou'd conserve my good opinion with her.

Sir Pat.
Ah, what a blessing I possess in so excellent a Wife! and in regard I am every day descending to my Grave,—ah— I will no longer hide from thee the provision I have made for thee, in case I die.—

La. Fa.
This is the Musick that I long'd to hear.—Die!—Oh that fatal word will kill me—*[Weeps.]* Name it no more if you'd preserve my life.—

Sir Pat.
Hah,—now cannot I refrain joyning with her in affectionate tears— no but do not weep for me my excellent Lady —for I have made a pretty competent Estate for thee, Eight thousand Pounds, which I have conceal'd in my Study behind the Wainscot on the left hand as you come in.

La. Fa.
Oh tell not me of transitory wealth, for I'me resolv'd not to survive thee, Eight thousand Pounds say you?—Oh I cannot indure the thoughts on't.

[Weeps.

Sir Pat.
Eight thousand Pounds just, my dearest Lady.

La. Fa.
Oh you'l make me desperate in naming it,—is it in Gold or Silver?

Sir Pat.
In Gold my Dearest the most-part, the rest in Silver.

La. Fa.
Good Heavens! why shou'd you take such pleasure in afflicting me. *[Weeps.]*—Behind the Wainscot say you?

Sir Pat.
Behind the Wainscot, prethee be pacifi'd,—thou makest me lose my greatest vertue, Moderation, to see thee thus, alas we're all born to die.—

La. Fa.
Again of dying! uncharitable man, why do you delight in tormenting me?—on the left hand say you as you go in?

Sir Pat.
On the left hand my Love, had ever Man such a Wife?

La. Fa.
Oh my Spirits fail me,—lead me, or I shall faint,— lead me to the Study and shew me where 'tis,—for I am able to hear no more of it.

Sir Pat.
I will, if you will promise indeed and indeed, not to grieve too much.

[Going to lead her out.
Enter Wittmore.

Witt.
Heaven grant me some kind opportunity to speak with *Lucia*! hah, she's here,—and with her the fond Cuckold her Husband,—Death, he has spy'd me, there's no avoiding him.—

Sir Pat.
Oh, are you there Sir?—*Maundy* look to my Lady, —I take it Sir, you have not dealt well with a person of my Authority and Gravity.

[Gropes for the Letter in his pocket.

Witt.
So, this can be nothing less than my being found out to be no *Yorkshire* Esq;: a Pox of my *Geneva* breeding, it must be so, what the Devil shall I say now?

Sir Pat.
And this disingenuous dealing does ill become the person you have represented, I take it.

Sir Patient Fancy

Witt.
Represented! Aye there 'tis, wou'd I were handsomely off o' this business; neither *Lucia* nor *Maundy* have any intelligence in their demure looks that can instruct a man,—why faith Sir,—I must confess,—I am to blame—and that I have—a—

La. Fa.
Oh *Maundy*! he'l discover all, what shall we do?

Sir Pat.
Have what Sir?

VVitt.
From my violent passion for your Daughter.—

La. Fa.
Oh I'me all confusion.—

VVitt.
Egad I am i'th' wrong, I see by *Lucia*'s looks.

Sir Pat.
That you have Sir, you wou'd say, made a sport and May-game of the ingagement of your word; I take it Mr. *Fain-love*, 'tis not like the stock you came from.

VVitt.
Yes, I was like to have spoil'd all, 'sheart what fine work I had made—but most certainly he has discover'd my passion for his Wife,—well, Impudence assist me—I made Sir a trifle of my word Sir, from whom have you this intelligence?

Sir Pat.
From whom shou'd I Sir, but from my Daughter *Isabella*?

Witt.
Isabella! The malicious Baggage understood to whom my first Courtship was address'd last night, and has betray'd me.

Sir Pat.
And Sir to let you see I utter nothing without precaution, pray read that Letter.

VVitt.
Hah—a Letter! what can this mean,—'tis *Lucia*'s hand, with *Isabella*'s name to't,—Oh the dear cunning Creature to make her Husband the messenger too. *[He Reads]*—How, I send one in my room?

La. Fa.
Yes Sir, you think we do not know of the appointment you made last night, but having other affairs in hand than to keep your promise, you sent Mr. *Knowel* in your room,—false man.

VVitt.
I send him Madam! I wou'd have sooner died.

Sir Pat.
Sir as I take it he cou'd not have known of your designes and Rendezvous without your information,—were not you to have met my Daughter here to night Sir?

VVitt.
Yes Sir, and I hope 'tis no such great crime, to desire a little conversation with the fair person one loves, and is so soon to marry, which I was hinder'd from doing by the greatest and most unlucky misfortune that ever arriv'd: but for my sending him, Madam, credit me, there's nothing so much amazes me and afflicts me, as to know he was here.

Sir Pat.
He speaks well, ingenuously he do's,—well Sir for your Father's sake, whose memory I reverence, I will for once forgive you, but let's have no more night-works, no more Gamballs I beseech you good Mr. *Fain-love.*

VVitt.
I humbly thank ye Sir, and do beseech you to tell the dear Creature that writ this, that I love her more than life or fortune, and that I wou'd sooner have kill'd the man that usurp'd my place last night than have assisted him.

La. Fa.
Were you not false then?—Now hang me if I do not credit him.

[Aside.

Sir Pat.
Alas good Lady! how she's concern'd for my Interest, she's even jealous for my Daughter.

[Aside.

VVitt.
False! charge me not with unprofitable sins; wou'd I refuse a Blessing, or blaspheme a Power that might undo me? wou'd I die in my full vigorous health, or live in constant pain? All this I cou'd, sooner than be untrue.

Sir Pat.
Ingenuously, my Lady *Fancy*, he speaks discreetly, and to purpose.

La. Fa.
Indeed my Dear he does, and like an honest Gentleman, and I shou'd think my self very unreasonable not to believe him,—and Sir I'le undertake your peace shall be made with your Mistress.

Sir Pat.
Well, I am the most fortunate man in a Wife that ever had the blessing of a good one.

VVitt.
Madam, let me fall at your feet, and thank you for this Bounty. [*Kneels.*]—Make it your own case, and then consider what returns ought to be made to the most passionate and faithful of Lovers.

Sir Pat.
I profess, a wonderful good natur'd youth this, rise Sir, my Lady *Fancy* shall do you all the kind Offices she can, o' my word she shall.

La. Fa.
I'me all obedience Sir, and doubtless shall obey you.

Sir Pat.
You must, indeed you must, and Sir I'le defer your Happiness no longer, this day you shall be marry'd.

Witt.
This day Sir!—why, the Writings are not made.

Sir Pat.
No matter Mr. *Fainlove*, her Portion shall be equivalent to the Jointure you shall make her, I take it, that's sufficient.

Witt.
A Jointure quoth he! it must be in New *Eutopian* Land then,—and must I depart thus, without a kind word, a look, or a billiet, to signify what I am to expect?

Looking on her slily.

Sir Pat.
Come, my Lady *Fancy*, shall I wait on you down to Prayer? Sir you will go get your self in order for your Marriage, the great affair of human life, I must to my mornings Devotion: come Madam.

She endeavours to make signs to Wittmore.

La. Fa.
Alas Sir, the sad discourse you lately made me, has so disorder'd me, and given me such a pain in my head, I am not able to endure the Psalm singing.

Sir Pat.
This comes of your weeping,—but we'l omit that part of th'exercise, and have no Psalm sung.

La. Fa.
Oh by no means Sir, 'twill scandalize the Brethren, for you know a Psalm is not sung so much out of devotion as 'tis to give notice of our Zeal and Pious intentions, 'tis a kind of Proclamation to the Neighbour-hood, and cannot be omitted, —Oh how my head aches!

Witt.
He were a damn'd dull Lover that cou'd not guess what she meant by this.

[Aside.

Sir Pat.
Well, my Lady *Fancy*, your Ladiship shall be obey'd, —come Sir, we'l leave her to her Women.

[Ex. Sir Pat.

Sir Patient Fancy

As Wittmore goes out, he bows and looks on her, she gives him a sign.

Witt.
That kind look is a sufficient invitation.—

La. Fa.
Maundy follow 'em down, and bring *Wittmore* back again,—*[Exit Maund.]* There's now a necessity of our contriving to avoid this marriage handsomely,—and we shall at least make two hours our own, I never wish'd well to long Prayers till this minute.
Enter Wittmore.

Witt.
Oh my dear *Lucia*!

La. Fa.
Oh *Wittmore*! I long to tell thee what a fatal mistake had like to have happen'd last night.

Witt.
My friend has told me all, and how he was prevented by the coming of your Husband from robbing me of those sacred delights I languish for, oh let us not lose inestimable time in dull talking, but haste to give each other the only confirmation we can give, how little we are our own.

La. Fa.
I see *Lodwick*'s a Man of Honour, and deserves a heart if I had one to give him.

[Exeunt.

SCENE III.
A Hall.

Enter Sir Patient and Roger.

Sir Pat.
Roger, is Prayer ready, *Roger*?

Rog.
Truely nay Sir, for Mr. *Gogle* hath taken too much of the Creature this Morning, and is not in case, Sir.

Sir Pat.
How mean you Sirrah, that Mr. *Gogle* is overtaken with Drink?

Rog.
Nay Sir, he hath over-eaten himself at Breakfast only.

Sir Pat.
Alas and that's soon done, for he hath a sickly Stomach as well as I, poor man—where is *Bartholomew*, the Clerk, he must hold forth then to day.

Rog.
Verily he is also disabled, for going forth last night by your commandment to smite the wicked, he received a blow over the *Pericranium.—*

Sir Pat.
Why how now Sirrah, Latin! the Language of the Beast! hah—and what then Sir?

Rog.
Which blow I doubt Sir, hath spoiled both his Praying and his Eating.
Sir Pat.
Hah! what a Family's here? no prayer to day!

Enter Nurse and Fanny.

Nurs.
Nay verily it shall all out, I will be no more the dark lanthorn to the deeds of darkness.

Sir Pat.
What's the matter here?

Nurs.
Sir, this young Sinner has long been privy to all the daily and nightly meetings between Mr. *Lodwick* and *Isabella*, and just now I took her tying a letter to a string in the Garden which he drew up to his Window, and I have born it till my Conscience will bear it no longer.

Sir Pat.
Hah, so young a Bawd!—tell me Minion,—private meeting! tell me truth I charge ye, when? where? how? and how often? oh she's debauch't!—her reputation's ruin'd, and she'le need a double Portion. Come tell me truth, for this little Finger here has told me all.

Fan.
Oh Geminy Sir, then that little Finger's the hougesest great Lyer as ever was.

Sir Pat.
Huzy huzy—I will have thee whipt most unmercifully: *Nurse* fetch me the Rod.

Fan.
Oh pardon me Sir this one time and I'le tell all.

[Kneels.

—Sir—I have seen him in the Garden, but not very often.
Sir Pat.

Often! oh, my Family's dishonoured, tell me truly what he us'd to do there—or I will have thee whipt without cessation, oh I'me in a cold Sweat, there's my fine Maid, was he with her long?

Fan.
Long enough.

Sir Pat.
Long enough!—oh 'tis so, long enough—for what, hah? my dainty Miss, tell me, and didst thou leave 'em?

Fan.
They us'd to send me to gather flowers to make Nose-gays Sir.

Sir Pat.
Ah, demonstration, 'tis evident if they were left alone that they were naught, I know't,—and where were they the while? in the close Arbour?—Aye Aye—I will have it cut down, it is the Pent-house of Iniquity, the very Coverlid of Sin.

Fan.
No Sir, they sat on the Primrose Bank.

Sir Pat.
What, did they sit all the while, or stand—or—lye —or—oh how was't?

Fan.
They only sat indeed Sir Father.

Sir Pat.
And thou didst not hear a word they said all the while?

Fan.
Yes I did Sir, and the man talkt a great deal of this, and of that, and of t'other, and all the while threw Jesimine in her bosome.

Sir Pat.
Well said, and did he nothing else?

Fan.
No indeed, Sir Father, nothing.

Sir Pat.
But what did she say to the man again?

Fan.
She said, let me see,—Aye she said, Lord you'le forget your self, and stay till somebody catch us.

Sir Pat.
Ah, very fine,—then what said he?

Fan.
Then he said, Well if I must be gon, let me leave thee with this hearty curse, A Pox take thee all over for making me love thee so confoundedly.

Sir Pat.
Oh horrible!

Fan.
—Oh I cou'd live here forever,—that was when he kist her—her hand only, are you not a Damn'd woman for making so fond a Puppy of me?

Sir Pat.
Oh unheard of wickedness!

Fan.
Wou'd the Devil had thee and all thy family, e're I had seen thy Cursed face.

Sir Pat.
Oh I'le hear no more,—I'le hear no more—why what a Blasphemous wretch is this!

Fan.
Pray Sir Father, do not tell my Sister of this, she'le be horribly angry with me.

Sir Pat.
No no, get you gon,—oh I am heart-sick—I'le up and consult with my Lady what's fit to be done in this affair, oh never was the like heard of.—

Goes out, Fanny goes the other way.

Scene, the Lady Fancies Bedchamber, she's discovered with Wittmore in disorder. A Table, Sword, and Hatt.

Maun.
O Madam, Sir *Patient*'s coming up.

La. Fan.
Coming up say you!

Sir Patient Fancy

Maun.
He's almost on the top of the Stairs, Madam.

Witt.
What shall I doe?

La. Fa.
Oh Damn him, I know not, if he see thee here after my pretended Illness, he must needs discover why I feign'd,—I have no Excuse ready,—this Chamber's unlucky, there's no avoiding him, here—step behind the Bed, perhaps he has only forgot his Psalm Book and will not stay long.

Wittmore runs behind the Bed.
Enter Sir Patient.

Sir Pat.
Oh, oh, pardon this interruption my Lady *Fancy* —oh I am half kill'd, my Daughter, my Honour—my Daughter, my Reputation.

La. Fa.
Good Heavens Sir, is she dead?

Sir Pat.
I wou'd she were, her Portion and her Honour wou'd then be sav'd, but oh I'me sick at heart, *Maundy*, fetch me the Bottle of *Mirabilis* in the Closet,—she's wanton—unchast,

Enter Maundy with the Bottle.

oh I cannot speak it, oh the Bottle—*[Drinks]* she has lost her Fame,—her Shame—her Name—oh *[Drinks]* this is not the right Bottle—that with the red Cork *[Drinks]*

[Ex. Maundy —and is grown a very t'other end of the town Creature, a very Apple of *Sodom*, fair without and filthy within, what shall we

Enter Maundy.

doe with her? she's lost, undone; *[Drinks]* hah—let me see, *[Drinks]* this is—*[Drinks]* not as I take it—*[Drinks]* —no— 'tis not the right—she's naught,—she's lewd,—*[Drinks]* — oh how you Vex me—*[Drinks]* this is not the right Bottle, yet—*[Drinks]* no no—here.

[Gives her the Bottle.

Maun.
You said, that with the Red Cork Sir.

[Goes out.

Sir Pat.
I meant the Blew,—I know not what I say,—in fine, my Lady let us marry her out of hand, for she is fall'n, fall'n to Perdition; she understands more wickedness then had she been bred in a profane Nunnery—a Court, or a Play-house,

Enter Maundy.

[Drinks]—therefore let's Marry her instantly—out of hand, *[Drinks]* Misfortune on Misfortune, *[Drinks]*—but Patience is a wonderfull Vertue, *[Drinks]*—ha—this is very Comfortable, —very Consoling,—I profess if it were not for these Creature ravishing Comforts, sometimes, a Man were a very odd sort of an Animal *[Drinks]* but ah—see how all things were ordain'd for the use and comfort of man *[Drinks.]*

La. Fa.
I like this well; Ah Sir 'tis very true, therefore receive it plentifully and thankfully.

Sir Pat. Drinks]
Ingeniously—it hath made me marvellous lightsome,—I profess it hath a very notable Faculty, —very knavish—and as—it were—waggish,—but —hah—what have we there on the Table? a Sword and Hat?

Sir Patient Fancy

Sees Wittmore's Sword and Hat on the Table which he had forgot.

La. Fa.
Curse on my Dullness,—oh—these Sir, they are Mr. *Fainloves* —he being so soon to be Marry'd, and being straitned for time, sent these to *Maundy* to be new trim'd with Ribbon Sir—that's all,—take 'em away you naughty Baggage, must I have mens things seen in my Chamber?

Sir Pat.
Nay nay, be not angry my little Rogue, I like the young mans frugality well,—go go your ways,—get you gon—and finefy your knacks, and tranghams, and do your business—goe.—

Smiling on Maundy, gently beating her with his hand: she goes out, he bolts the door after her, and sits down on the Beds feet.

La. Fa.
Heavens, what means he!

Sir Pat.
Come hither to me my little Apes face,—come —come I say—what must I come fetch you?—Catch her, catch her, catch her—catch her, catch her, catch her.

Running after her.

La. Fa.
Oh Sir I am so ill I can hardly stir.

Sir Pat.
I'le make ye well, come hither ye Monky face, did it, did it, did it? alas for it, a poor silly fools face, dive it a blow and I'le beat it.

La. Fa.
You neglect your Devotion Sir.

Sir Pat.
No no, no Prayer to day my little Rascall,—no Prayer to day—poor *Gogle*'s sick—come hither—why you Refractory Baggage you, come or I shall touze you, ingenuously I shall, tom tom or I'le whip it.

La. Fa.
Have you forgot your Daughter Sir? and your disgrace?
Sir Pat.
A fiddle on my Daughter, she's a Chick of the old Cock I profess, I was just such another wag when young,—but she shall be marry'd to morrow, a good Cloke for her knavery; therefore come your ways, ye wag, we'le take a nap together, good faith my little Harlot I mean thee no harm.

La. Fa.
No o' my Conscience.—

Sir Pat.
Why then, why then you little Mungrel?

La. Fa.
His precise worship is as it were disguis'd, the outward man is overtaken—pray Sir lye down, and I'le come to you presently.

Sir Pat.
Away you wag, will you? will you—catch her there, catch her.

La. Fa.
I will indeed—death there's no getting from him,—pray lye down—and I'le cover thee close enough I'le warrant thee.—

[*Aside.*

He lyes down, she covers him. Had ever Lovers such spightfull Luck? hah—surely he sleeps, bless the mistaken Bottle—Aye, he sleeps,—whist, *Wittmore* .—

He coming out falls: pulls the Chair down, Sir Patient flings open the Curtain.

Witt.
Plague of my over Care, what shall I doe?

Sir Pat.
What's that, what noise is that? let me see, we are not safe, lock up the doors, what's the matter, what Thunder Clap was that?

Wittmore runs under the Bed: she runs to Sir Patient and holds him in his Bed.

La. Fa.
Pray Sir lye still, 'twas I was only going to sit down, and a suddain giddiness took me in my head which made me fall and with me the Chair, there is no danger near ye Sir—I was just coming to sleep by you.

Sir Pat.
Go you 're a flattering Huswife, goe, Catch her, catch her—catch her.—

[*Lyes down, she covers him.*

La. Fa.
Oh how I tremble at the dismal apprehension of being discovered, had I secur'd my self of the Eight thousand Pound, I wou'd not value *Wittmores* being seen, but now to be found out wou'd call my Wit in question, for 'tis the fortunate alone are wise.—

Wittmore peeps from under the Bed: she goes softly to the door to open it.

Witt.
Was ever man so Plagu'd?—hah—what's this? —confound my tell-tale Watch, the Larum goes, and there's no getting to't to silence it;—Damn'd Misfortune!

> [*Sir Patient rises and flings open the Curtains.*

Sir Pat.
Hah, what's that!

La. Fa.
Heavens! what's the matter? we are destin'd to discovery.

> [*She runs to Sir Patient, and leaves the door still fast.*

Sir Pat.
What's that I say, what's that? let me see, let me see, what ringing's that, oh let me see what 'tis.

> [*Strives to get up, she holds him down.*

La. Fa.
Oh now I see my fate's inevitable, alas that ever I was born to see't.

> [*Weeps.*

Witt.
Death she'le tell him I am here! nay he must know't, a Pox of all invention and Mechanicks, and he were damn'd that first contriv'd a Watch.

Sir Pat.
Hah, dost weep,—why dost weep? I say what noise is that? what ringing? hah.—

La. Fa.
'Tis that, 'tis that my dear that makes me weep, alas I never hear this fatall Noise but some dear friend dyes.

Sir Pat.
Hah, dyes! oh that must be I, Aye Aye, oh.

La. Fa.
I've heard it Sir this two dayes, but wou'd not tell you of it.

Sir Pat.
Hah! heard it these two dayes? oh, what is't, a death-watch?—hah.—

La. Fa.
Aye Sir, a death-watch, a certain Larum death-watch, a thing that has warn'd our Family this hundred years, oh—I'me the most undone Woman.

Witt.
A blessing on her for a dear dissembling Gilt—death and the Devil, will it never cease?

Sir Pat.
A death-watch? ah, 'tis so, I've often heard of these things— methinks it sounds as if 'twere under the Bed.—

> *[Offers to look, she holds him.*

La. Fa.
You think so Sir, but that 'tis about the Bed is my grief, it therefore threatens you: oh wretched Woman!

Sir Pat.
Aye, aye, I'me too happy in a wife to live long: well, I will settle my House at *Hogsdowne* with the Land about it, which is 500 l. a year upon thee, live or dye, — do not grieve. —

[Lays himself down.

La. Fa.
Oh I never had more cause, come try to sleep; your fate may be diverted — whilst I'le to prayers for your dear health, — I have almost run
[Covers him, draws the Curtains. out all my stock of Hypocrisie, and that hated Art now fails me, — oh all ye Powers that favour distrest Lovers, assist us now, and I'le provide against your future Malice.

She makes signes to Wittmore, he peeps.

Witt.
I'me impatient of Freedom, yet so much happiness as I but now injoy'd without this part of Suffering had made me too blest, — Death and Damnation! what curst luck have I?

Makes signs to her to open the Door: whilst he creeps softly from under the Bed to the Table, by which going to raise himself he pulls down all the Dressing things: at the same instant Sir Patient leaps from the Bed, and she returns from the door and sits on Wittmores back as he lies on his hands and knees, and makes as if she swounded.

Sir Pat.
What's the matter! what's the matter! has *Satan* broke his everlasting Chain and got loose abroad to Plague poor Mortalls? hah — what's the matter?

[Runs to his Lady.

La. Fa.
Oh help, I dye, — I faint — run down and call for help.

Sir Patient Fancy

Sir Pat.
My Lady dying? oh she's gon, she faints,—what ho, who waits?

[*Cries and baules.*

La. Fa.
Oh, go down and bring me help, the door is lockt, —they cannot hear ye—oh—I goe—I dye.—

[*He opens the door and calls help, help.*

Witt.
Damn him! there's no escaping without I kill the Dog.

[*from under her, peeping.*

La. Fa.

    Lye still or we are undone.—
    Sir Patient returns with Maundy.

Maun.
Hah, discover'd!

Sir Pat.
Help, help my Lady dies.—

Maun.
Oh I perceive how 'tis—Alas she's dead, quite gone, oh rub her temples Sir.

Sir Pat.
Oh I'me undone then,—[*Weeps*] oh my dear, my Vertuous Lady?—

Sir Patient Fancy

La. Fa.
Oh where's my Husband, my dearest Husband—oh bring him near me.

Sir Pat.
I'me here my Excellent Lady.—

She takes him about the neck and raises her self up, gives Wittmore a little kick behind.

Witt.
Oh the dear Lovely Hypocrite, was ever Man so near discovery?—

[*Goes out.*

Sir Pat.
Oh how hard she presses my head to her Bosome!

Maun.
Ah, that grasping hard Sir, is a very bad sign.

Sir Pat.
How does my good, my dearest Lady *Fancy*?

La. Fa.
Something better now, give me more Air,—that dismall Larum Death-watch had almost kill'd me.

Sir Pat.
Ah Precious Creature, how she afflicts her self for me,—come let's walk into the Dining room, 'tis more Airie, from thence into my Study, and make thy self Mistress of that Fortune I have design'd thee, thou best of Women.

[*Exeunt, Leading her.*

The End of the Fourth Act.

Sir Patient Fancy

ACT V.

SCENE I.

A Table, and Six Chairs.

Enter Isabella Reading a Letter, Betty tricking her.

Isab.
How came you by this Letter?

Bet.
Miss *Fanny* receiv'd it by a string from his Window, by which he took up that you writ to him this morning.

Isab.
What means this nicety? forbear I say.—

[*puts Betty from her.*

Bet.
You cannot be too fine upon your VVedding day.

Isab.
Thou art mistaken, leave me,—whatever he says here to satisfy my jealousy, I am confirm'd that he was false, yet this assurance to free me from this intended marriage, makes me resolve to pardon him however guilty.—

Enter Wittmore.

How now! what means this insolence? How dare you having so lately made your guilty approaches, venture again into my presence?

Witt.
Why? Is there any danger, but what's so visible, in those fair eyes?

Isab.
And there may lie enough Sir, when they're angry. By what Authority do you make this sawcy visit?

Witt.
That of a Husband Madam, I came to congratulate the mighty joy this day will bring you.

Isab.
Thou dar'st not marry me, there will be danger in't.

Witt.
Why sure you do not carry Death in your imbraces, I find no Terrour in that lovely shape, no Daggers in that pretty scornfull look; that breath that utters so much Anger now, last night was sweet as new-blown Roses are,—and spoke such words, so tender and so kind.

Isab.
And canst thou think they were address'd to thee?

Witt.
No, nor cou'd the shade of Night hide the confusion which disorder'd you, at the discovery that I was not he, the blessed he you look'd for.

Isab.
Leave me, thou hated object of my Soul.

VVitt.
This will not serve your turn, for I must marry you.

Isab.
Then thou art a fool, and drawest thy ruin on; why I will hate thee,— hate thee most extreamly.

VVitt.
That will not anger me.

Isab.
Why, I will never let thee touch me, not kiss my hand, not come into my sight.

VVitt.
Are there no other women, kind, fair, and to be purchas'd? he cannot starve for Beauty in this age, that has a stock to buy.

Isab.
Why, I will Cuckold thee, look to't; I will most damnably.

VVitt.
So wou'd you, had you lov'd me, in a year or two; therefore like a kind civil Husband I've made provision for you, a friend, and one I dare trust my Honour with,—'tis Mr. *Knowel*, Madam.

Isab.
Lodwick! What Devil brought that name to his knowledge?—canst thou know him, and yet dare hope to marry me?

VVitt.
We have agree'd it, and on these conditions.

Isab.
Thou basely injurest him, he cannot do a deed he ought to blush for: *Lodwick* do this! Oh do not credit it,—prethee be just and kind for thy own Honours sake, be quickly so, the hasty minutes fly, and will anon make up the fatal hour that will undoe me.

VVitt.
'Tis true, within an hour you must submit to *Hymen*, there's no avoiding it.

Isab.
Nay then be gone my poor submissive Prayers, and all that dull Obedience custom has made us slaves to,—do, Sacrifice me, lead me to the Altar, and see if all the holy mystick words can Conjure from me the consenting syllable: No, I will not add one word to make the charm compleat, but stand as silent in th'inchanting Circle, as if the Priests were raising Devils there.
Enter Lodwick.

Lod.
Enough, enough, my charming *Isabella*, I am confirm'd.

Isab.
Lodwick! what good Angel conducted thee hither?

Lod.
E'en honest *Charles VVittmore* here, thy friend and mine, no Bug-bear Lover he!

Isab.
VVittmore! that friend I've often heard thee name? now some kind mischief on him, he has so frighted me, I scarce can bring my sense to so much order, to thank him that he loves me not.

Lod.
Thou shalt defer that payment to more leisure, we're men of business now. My Mother knowing of a Consultation of Physicians which your Father has this day appointed to meet at his house, has brib'd Monsieur *Turboone*, his *French* Doctor in Pension, to admit of a Doctor or two of her recommending, who shall amuse him with discourse till we get our selves married; and to make it the more ridiculous, I will release Sir *Credulous* from the Basket, I saw it in the Hall as I came through, we shall have need of the fool.

[*Ex. Witt.*

Enter Wittmore pulling in the Basket.

Witt.
'Twill do well.

Lod.
Sir *Credulous* how is't man?

[Opens the Basket.

Sir Cred.
What am not I at the Carriers yet?—Oh *Lodwick* thy hand, I'me almost poison'd—this Basket wants airing extreamly, it smells like an old Ladies Wedding-Gown of my acquaintance,—but what's the danger past, man?

Lod.
No, but there's a necessity of your being for some time disguis'd to act a Physician.

Sir Cred.
How! a Physician! that I can easily do, for I understand Simples.

Lod.
That's not material, so you can but Banter well, be very Grave, and put on a starch'd countenance.

Sir Cred.
Banter? what's that, man?

Lod.
Why Sir, talking very much, and meaning just nothing; be full of words without any connexion, sence, or conclusion: come in with me, and I'le instruct you farther.

Sir Cred.
Pshaw, is that all, say no more ont, I'le do't, let me alone for Bantering,—but this same damn'd Rival?—

Lod.
He's now watching for you without, and means to souce upon you, but trust to me for your security, come away, I have your habit ready. *[Goes out.]*—This day shall make thee mine, Dear *Isabella* .—

[*Ex. Lod. and Witt.*

Enter Sir Patient, and Leander, and Roger.

Sir Pat.
Marry *Lucretia*! is there no Woman in the City fit for you but the Daughter of the most notorious fantastical Lady within the Walls?

Lean.
Yet that fantastical Lady you thought fit for a Wife for me Sir.

Sir Pat.
Yes Sir, Foppery with Money had been something, but a poor Fop, hang't 'tis abominable.

Lean.
Pray hear me Sir.

Sir Pat.
Sirrah, Sirrah, you're a Jackanapes, ingenuously you are Sir, Marry *Lucretia* quoth he!

Lean.
If it were so Sir, where's her fault?

Sir Pat.
Why Mr. Coxcombe, all over. Did I with so much care endeavour to marry thee to the Mother, only to give thee opportunity with *Lucretia*?
Enter Lady Knowel.

Lean.
This Anger shews your great concern for me.

Sir Pat.
For my name I am, but 'twere no matter if thou wert hang'd, and thou deservest it for thy lewd Cavaliering Opinion,—they say thou art a Papist too, or at least a Church of *England* Man, and I profess there's not a pin to chuse,— Marry *Lucretia*!

La. Kn.
Were I querimonious, I shou'd resent the affront this *Balatroon* has offer'd me.

Isab.
Dear Madam, for my sake do not anger him now.

[*Aside to her.*

La. Kn.
Upon my Honour you are very free with my Daughter Sir.

Sir Pat.
How! she here! now for a Peal from her eternal Clapper, I had rather be confin'd to an Iron-mill.

La. Kn.
Sure *Lucretia* merits a Husband of as much worth as your Nephew Sir.

Sir Pat.
A better, Madam, for he's the lewdest Hector in the Town, he has all the Vices of youth, Whoring, Swearing, Drinking, Damning, Fighting,—and a Thousand more, numberless and nameless.

La. Kn.
Time Sir may make him more abstemious.

Sir Pat.
Oh never Madam! 'tis in's Nature, he was born with it, he's given over to Reprobation, 'tis bred i'th' bone,—he's lost.

Lean.
This is the first good Office that ever he did me.

La. Kn.
What think you Sir, if in defiance of your Inurbanity, I take him with all these faults my self?

Sir Pat.
How Madam!

La. Kn.
Without more Ambages Sir, I have consider'd your former desires, and have consented to marry him, notwithstanding your exprobrations.

Sir. Pat.
May I believe this Madam, and has your Ladiship that goodness!— and hast thou my Boy so much Wit? why this is something now,— well he was ever the best and sweetest natur'd youth,—why what a notable wag's this? and is it true my Boy, hah?

Lean.
Yes Sir, I had told you so before had you permitted me to speak.

Sir Pat.
Well Madam, he is onely fit for your excellent Ladiship, he is the prettiest civillest Lad!—well go thy ways; I shall never see the like of thee, no—Ingeniously the Boy's made for ever, Two thousand Pounds a year besides Money, Plate, and Jewels, made for ever.—Well Madam, the satisfaction I take in this Alliance, has made me resolve to give him immediately my Writings of all my Land in *Berkshire* , Five hundred Pounds a year Madam, and I wou'd have you Married this morning with my Daughter, so one Dinner and one Rejoycing will serve both.

La. Kn.
That Sir, we have already agree'd upon.

Sir Pat.
Well I'le fetch the Writings. Come *Isabella*, I'le not trust you out of my sight to day.

[*Ex. Sir Pat. and Isab.*

Lean.
VVell then Madam, you are resolv'd upon this business of Matrimony.

La. Kn.
Was it not concluded between us Sir this morning? and at the near approach do you begin to fear?

Lean.
Nothing Madam, since I'me convinc'd of your goodness.

La. Kn.
You flatter Sir, this is meer Adulation.

Lean.
No, I am that wild Extravagant my Uncle render'd me, and cannot live confin'd.

La. Kn.
To one Woman you mean? I shall not stand with you for a Mistress or two, I hate a dull morose unfashionable Blockhead to my Husband, nor shall I be the first example of a suffering Wife Sir; Women were created poor obedient things.

Lean.
And can you be content to spare me five or six-nights in a week?

La. Kn.
Oh you're too reasonable.

Lean.
And for the rest, if I get drunk, perhaps I'le give to you: yet in my Drink I'me damn'd ill natur'd too, and may neglect my duty, perhaps shall be so wicked to call you cunning, deceitful, gilting, base, and swear you have undone me, swear you have ravish'd from my faithful heart, all that cou'd make it blest or happy.
Enter Lucretia weeping.

La. Fa.
How now *Lucretia*?

Lucr.
Oh Madam, give me leave to kneel before, and tell you if you pursue the Cruelty I hear you're going to commit, I am the most lost, most wretched Maid that breaths; We two have plighted faiths, and shou'd you marry him, 'twere so to sin as Heaven wou'd never pardon.

La. Kn.
Rise fool.

Lucr.
Never, till you have given me back *Leander*, or leave to live no more,—pray kill me Madam; and the same

> Flowers that deck your Nuptial-bed,
> Shall serve to strow my Herse, when I shall lie
> A dead cold witness of your Tyranny.

La. Kn.
Rise, I still design'd him yours.—I saw with pleasure Sir, your reclination from my addresses,—I have prov'd both your Passions, and 'twere unkind not to Crown 'em with the due præmium of each others merits.

[Gives her to Lean.

Lean.
Can Heaven and you agree to be so bountiful?

La. Kn.
Be not amaz'd at this turn, *Rotat omne fatum*,— but no more,—keep still that mask of Love we first put on, till you have gain'd the Writings, for I have no joy beyond cheating that filthy Uncle of thine,—*Lucretia* wipe your eyes, and prepare for *Hymen*, the hour draws near. *Thalessio, Thalessio!* as the *Romans* cry'd.

Lucr.

> May you be still admir'd as you deserve!
> *Enter Sir Patient with Writings, and Isabella.*

Sir Pat.
How Madam *Lucretia*, and in tears!

La. Kn.
A little disgusted Sir, with her Father-in-law, Sir.

Sir Pat.
Oh is that all, hold up thy head Sweet-heart, thy turn's next,—here Madam, I surrender my Title, with these Writings, and with 'em my Joy, my Life, my Darling, my *Leander*,— now let's away, where's Mr. *Fain-love*?

Isab.
He's but stept into *Cheapside* to fit the Ring Sir, and will be here immediately.

Sir Pat.
I have business anon about Eleven of the Clock, a Consultation of Physicians to confer about this Carkase of mine.

Lean.
Physicians Sir, what to doe?

Sir Pat.
To do! why to take their advice Sir, and to follow it.

Lean.
For what I beseech you Sir?

Sir Pat.
Why Sir for my health.

Lean.
I believe you are not sick Sir,—unless they make you so.

Sir Pat.
They make me so!—do you hear him Madam,— am not I sick Sir? not I, Sir *Patient Fancy* sick?

La. Kn.
He'le destroy my design,—how Mr. *Fancy*, not Sir *Patient* sick? or must he be incinerated before you'le credit it?

Sir Pat.
Aye Madam, I want but dying to undeceive him, and yet I am not sick!

Lean.
Sir I love your life, and wou'd not have you die with Fancy and Conceit.—

Sir Pat.
Fancy and Conceit! do but observe him Madam,— what do ye mean Sir, by Fancy and Conceit?

La. Kn.
He'le ruin all,—why Sir,—he means—

Sir Pat.
Nay let him alone, let him alone, (with your Ladiships pardon)— come Sir,—Fancy and Conceit, I take it, was the Question in debate,—

Lean.
I cannot prove this to you Sir, by force of Argument, but by demonstration I will, if you will banish all your couzening Quacks, and take my wholesome advice.

Sir Pat.
Do but hear him Madam, not prove it.

La. Kn.
Sir he means nothing,—not sick! alas Sir you're very sick.

Sir Pat.
Aye, Aye, your Ladiship is a Lady of profound knowledge—why have I not had the advice of all the Doctors in *England*, and have I not been in continual Physick this Twenty years,—and yet I am not sick! ask my dear Lady Sir, how sick I am, she can inform you.

[La. Kno. goes and talks to Isab.

Lean.
She does her endeavour Sir, to keep up the humour.

Sir Pat.
How Sir!

Lean.
She wishes you dead Sir.

Sir Pat.
What said the Rascal? wishes me dead!

Lean.
Sir she hates you.

Sir Pat.
How! hate me! what my Lady hate me?

Lean.
She abuses your Love, plays tricks with ye, and cheats ye Sir.

Sir Pat.
Was ever so prophane a wretch! what, you will not prove this neither?

Sir Patient Fancy

Lean.
Yes, by demonstration too.

Sir Pat.
Why thou sawcie Varlet, Sirrah, Sirrah thank my Lady here I do not cudgel thee, —well I will settle the rest of my Estate upon her to morrow, I will Sir, —and thank God you have what you have Sir, make much on't.

Lean.
Pardon me Sir, 'tis not my single opinion, but the whole City takes notice on't, that I tell it you Sir is the effects of my Duty not Interest, pray give me leave to prove this to you Sir.

Sir Pat.
What you are at your Demonstration again? —come —let's hear.

Lean.
Why Sir, —give her frequent opportunities, —and then surprise her, —or, —by pretending to settle all upon her, —give her your Power, and see if she do not turn you out of doors, —or —by feigning you are sick to death—or indeed by dying.

Sir Pat.
I thank you Sir, —this indeed is Demonstration, I take it.—

[*Pulls off his Hat.*

Lean.
I mean but feigning Sir, and be a witness your self of her sorrow, or contempt.

Sir Pat. Pauses]
—Hah—hum, —why ingeniously this may be a very pretty Project, —well Sir, suppose I follow your advice? —nay I profess I will do so, not to try her Faith, but to have the pleasure to hear

her Conjugal Lamentations, feel her Tears bedew my Face, and her sweet Mouth kissing my Cheeks a thousand times, verily a wonderful comfort,—and then Sir, what becomes of your Demonstration.—

Enter Wittmore with the Ring.

Oh,—Mr. *Fain-love,* come come you're tardy, let us away to Church.
Enter Roger.

Rog.
Sir here is Doctor *Turboone,* and those other Doctors your Worship expected.
Enter Lady Fancy.

Sir Pat.
The Doctors already!—well bring 'em up, come Madam, we have waited for your Ladiship,—bring up the Doctors *Roger.*

La. Fa.
Wittmore, I have now brought that design to a happy conclusion for which I married this formal Ass, I'le tell thee more anon,—we are observ'd.

La. Kn.
Oh *Lodwick's* come.
Enter Lodwick, Monsieur Turboon, Fat Doctor, Amsterdam, Leyden, Sir Credulous.

Sir Pat.
Doctor *Turboon* your Servant, I expected you not this two hours.

Turb.
Nor had ee com Sir, bot for dese wordy Gentelmen, whos affairs wode not permit dem to com at your hour.

Sir Pat.
Are they *English* pray?

Turb.
Dis is Sir,—*[pointing to Lod.]* an admirable Physician, and a rare Astrologer.—Dis speaks good *English*, bot a *Collender* born.

[points to Sir Cred.

Sir Cred.
What a pox does the Fellow call me a Cullender?

Lod.
He means a *High-Dutch* man of the Town of *Collen*, Sir.

Sir Pat.
Sir I have heard of your Fame,—Doctor pray entertain these Gentlemen till my return, I'le be with you presently.

Lod.
Sir I hope you go not forth to day?

[Gazing on his Face.

Sir Pat.
Not far, Sir.

Lod.
There is a certain Star has rul'd this two daies Sir, of a very malignant Influence to persons of your Complexion and constitution,—let me see—within this two hours and six Minutes, its Malice will be spent, till then it will be fatall.

Sir Pat.
Hum, reign'd this two days?—I profess and things have gon very cross with me this two daies,—a notable man this.

La. Kn.
Oh a very Profound Astrologer Sir, upon my Honour I know him.

Sir Pat.
But this is an affair of that importance Sir—

Lod.
If it be more than health or Life, I beg your Pardon Sir.

Sir Pat.
Nay no offence Sir I beseech you, I'le stay Sir.

La. Kn.
How! Sir *Patient* not see us Married?

Sir Pat.
You shall excuse me Madam.

La. Fa.
This was lucky, oh Madam wou'd you have my Dear venture out, when a malignant Star reigns! not for the world.

Sir Pat.
No I'le not stir, had it been any Star but a malignant Star, I had waited on your Ladiship. But these malignant Stars are very Pernicious stars. Nephew, take my Lady *Knowell*; Mr. *Fain-love* my Daughter, and *Bartholomew* do you conduct my Lady, the Parson stays for you, and the Coaches are at the door.

Exeunt Lady Knowell, Leander, Wittmore and

Isab. Lady Fancy and Bartholomew.

Enter Boy.

Boy.
Sir, my Lady has sent for you.

Lod.
Sir I'le be with you presently, Sir *Credulous* be sure you lug him by the Ears, with any sort of stuff, till my return, I'le send you a friend to keep you in Countenance.

Sir Pat.
Please you to sit Gentlemen?

Amst.
Please you Sir.

          [To Sir Cred. who bows and runs back.

Sir Cred.
Oh Lord sweet Sir, I hope you do not take me— Nay I beseech you Noble Sir—Reverend Sir.

          [Turning from one to t'other.

Leyd.
By no means Sir, a stranger.

Sir Cred.
I beseech you—*Scavantissimi Doctores,*—incomparable Sir,—and you—or you.

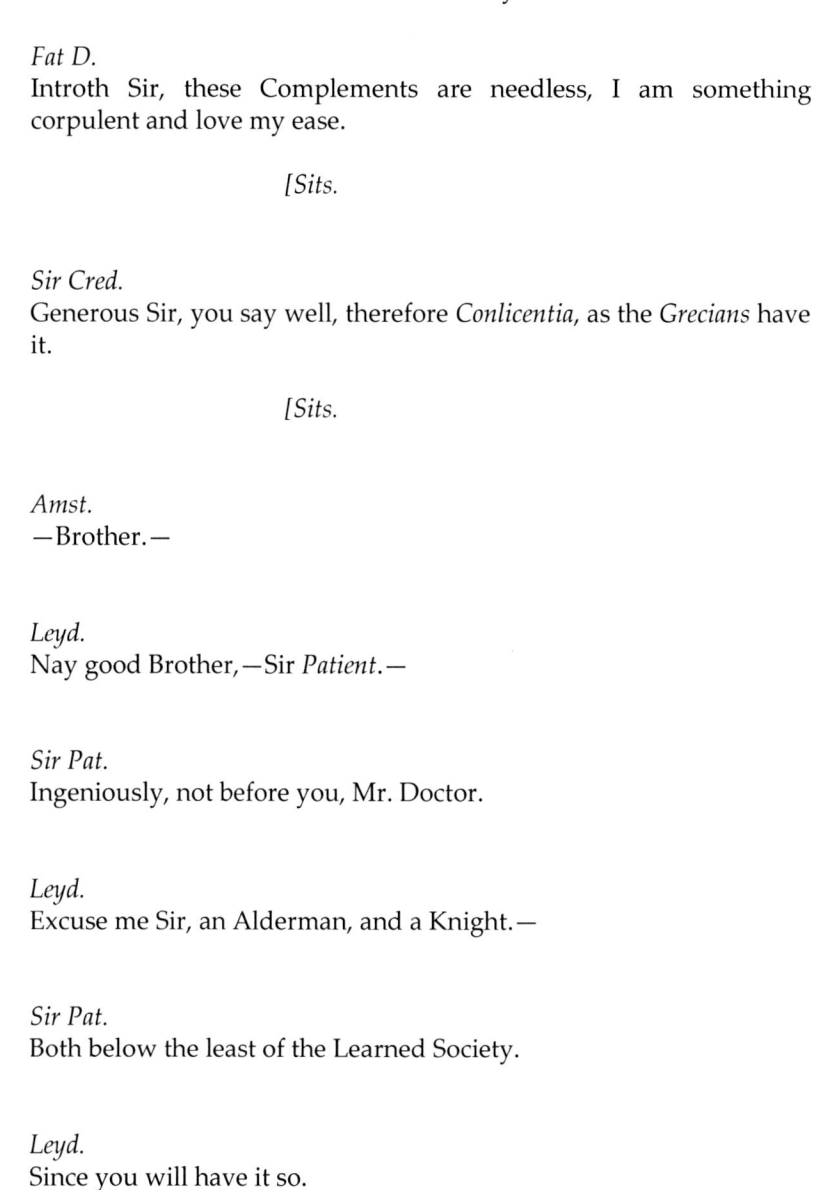

Fat D.
Introth Sir, these Complements are needless, I am something corpulent and love my ease.

[Sits.

Sir Cred.
Generous Sir, you say well, therefore *Conlicentia*, as the *Grecians* have it.

[Sits.

Amst.
—Brother.—

Leyd.
Nay good Brother,—Sir *Patient*.—

Sir Pat.
Ingeniously, not before you, Mr. Doctor.

Leyd.
Excuse me Sir, an Alderman, and a Knight.—

Sir Pat.
Both below the least of the Learned Society.

Leyd.
Since you will have it so.

All sit and cry hum,—and look gravely.

Sir Cred.
Hum—hum, most Worthy, and most Renouned— *Medicinæ Professores, qui hic assemblati estis; & vos altra Mesioris,* I am now going to make a Motion for the Publick good of us all, but will do nothing without your Doctorships Approbation.

Sir Pat.
Judiciously concluded.

Sir Cred.
The question then is, *Reverentisimi Doctores,* whether—for mark me, I come to the matter in hand, hating long Circumstances of words; there being no necessity as our Learned Brother *Rabalis* observes in that most notorious Treatise of his call'd *Garagantua* , there is says he, no necessity of going over the Hedg when the Path lies fair before ye; therefore as I said before, I now say again coming to my Question, for as that admirable *Welch* Divine says in that so famous Sermon of his, upon her Creat Cranfather Hadam and her Creat Cranmother Heeve concerning the Happell,—and her will warrant her, her will keep to her Text still,—so I stick close to my question, which is *Illustrissimi Doctores,* whether it be not necessary to the Affair in hand—to take—a Bottle, and if your Doctorships are of my opinion—hold up your Thumbs.

All hold up their Thumbs.

—Look Sir, you observe the Votes of the Learned *Cabalists.*

Sir Pat.
Which shall be put in Act forthwith—I like this man well, he does nothing without mature deliberation.

[Goes out.
Enter Brunswick.

Sir Patient Fancy

Brun.
By your leaves Gentlemen,—Sir *Credulous*—

[*Whispers.*

Sir Cred.
Oh—'tis *Ladwicks* Friend, the Rascall's drest like *Vanderbergen* in the *Strand*:—Sir *Patient*—pray know this glorious Doctor Sir.

Sir Pat.
A Doctor Sir?

Sir Cred.
A Doctor Sir, yes, and as Eloquent a Doctor, Sir, as ever set Bill to Post, why 'tis—the incomparable—*Brunswick*, high *Dutch* Doctor.

Sir Pat.
You're welcome Sir,—Pray sit; ah—well Sir you are come to visit a very Crazy sickly Person Sir.

Brun.
Pray let me feel your Pulse Sir,—what think you Gentlemen, is he not very far gone?—

[*Feels his pulse, they all feel.*

Sir Cred.
Ah far, far,—Pray Sir, have you not a certain wambling Pain in your Stomach Sir, as it were Sir a—a Pain Sir.

Sir Pat.
Oh very great Sir, especially in a Morning Fasting.

Sir Cred.
I knew it by your stinking breath Sir,—and are you not troubled with a pain in your Head Sir?

Sir Pat.
In my Head Sir?

Sir Cred.
I mean a—kind of a—Pain,—a kind of a—*Vertigo* as the *Latins* call it, and a *Whirligigoustiphon* as the *Greeks* have it, which signifies in *English* Sir, a Dizzie-swimming kind—of a de ye see—a thing—that—a—you understand me.

Sir Pat.
Oh intolerable, intolerable,—why this is a rare man.

Fat D.
Your reason Sir for that?

[To Sir Cred

Sir Cred.
My reason Sir? why my reason Sir is this, *Haly* the *Moore*, and *Rabbie Isack* and some thousands more of learned *Dutchmen* observe your dull wall Eye and your Whir— *Whirligigoustiphon,* to be inseparable.

Brun.
A most Learned reason.

Fat D.
Oh Sir inseparable.

Sir Cred.
And have you not a kind of a—something—de ye mark me, when you make water, a kind of a stopping—and— a—de ye conceive me, I have forgot the *English* term Sir, but in *Latin* 'tis a *Stronggullionibus.*

Sir Pat.
Oh Sir most extreamly, 'tis that which makes me desperate Sir.

Sir Cred.
Your ugly Face is an infallible sign, your *Dysurie* as the *Arabicks* call it, and your Ill-favor'd Countenance, are constant Relatives.

All.
Constant, constant.

Sir Cred.
Pray how do you eat, Sir?

Sir Pat.
Ah Sir, there's my distraction. Alas Sir, I have the weakest stomach—I do not make above four Meals a day, and then indeed I eat heartily—but alas what's that to eating to live,—nothing Sir nothing.—

Sir Cred.
Poor heart I pity him.

Sir Pat.
And between meals, good Wine, Sweet-meats, Caudles,—Cordialls and Mirabilises, to keep up my fainting Spirits.

Sir Cred.
A Pox of his Aldermanship: an the whole Bench were such notable swingers, twou'd Famish the City sooner than a Siege.

Amst.
Brothers what do you think of this man?

Leyd.
Think Sir? I think his Case is desperate.

Sir Cred.
Shaw Sir, we shall soon rectify the quiblets and quillities of his bloud if he observes our directions and diet, which is to eat but once in four or five daies.

Sir Pat.
How Sir, eat but once in four or five daies! such a dyet Sir wou'd kill me, alas Sir kill me.

Sir Cred.
Oh no Sir, no, for look ye Sir the Case is thus, do ye mind me—so that the business lying so obvious de ye see, there is a certain method do ye mark me—in a—Now Sir when a man goes about to alter the course of Nature,—the case is very plain, you may as well arrest the Chariot of the Sun, or alter the Eclipses of the Moon, for Sir this being of another Nature, the Nature of it is to be unnaturall, you conceive me Sir?—therefore we must crave your absence Sir for a few Minutes, till we have debated this great Affair.

Sir Pat.
With all my heart Sir, since my case is so desperate, a few hours were not too much.

[*Ex. Sir Patient.*]

Sir Cred.
Now Sir, my Service to you.

[*Drinks.*

Enter Fanny.

Fan.
Oh living heart! what do all these men do in our house? sure they are a sort of New-fashon'd *Conventiclers*:—I'le hear 'em preach.

[They drink round the while.

Amst.
Sir my service to you, and to your good Lady, Sir.

Ley.
Again to you Sir, not forgetting your Daughters: they are fine Women Sir, let Scandal do its worst.

[Drinks.

Turb.
To our better trading Sir.

Brun.
Faith it goes but badly on, I had the weekly Bill and 'twas a very thin Mortality, some of the better sort dye indeed that have good round Fees to give.

Turb.
Verily I have not kill'd above my five or six this week.

Brun.
How Sir kill'd?

Turb.
Kill'd Sir! ever whilst you live, especially those who have the grand *Verole*, for 'tis not for a man's Credit to let the Patient want an Eye or a Nose, or some other ting, I have kill'd ye my five or six dozen a week—but times are hard.

Brun.
I grant ye Sir, your Poor for Experiment, and improvement of Knowledge, and to say truth there ought to be such Scavengers as we to sweep away the Rubbish of the Nation.

[Sir Cred. and Fat seeming in discourse.

Sir Cred.
Nay an you talk of a beast; My service to you Sir— *[Drinks]* Aye, I lost the finest beast of a Mare in all *Devonshire*.

Fat D.
And I the finest Spaniel Sir.
*[Here they all talk together till you come to—*purpose Sir.

Turb.
Pray what news is there stirring?

Brun.
Faith Sir, I am one of those fools that never regard whether *Lewes* or *Philip* have the better or the worst.

Turb.
Peace is a great blessing Sir, a very great blessing.

Brun.
You are i'th' right Sir, and so my service to you Sir.

Ley.
Well, Sir, *Stetin* held out Nobly, though the Gazetts are various.

Amst.
There's a world of men kill'd they say, why what a shame 'tis so many thousand should dye without the help of a Physician.

Ley.
Hang 'em they were poor Rogues and not worth our killing, my service to you Sir, they'le serve to fill up Trenches.

Sir Cred.
Spaniell Sir! no man breathing understands Dogs and Horses better then my self.

Fat D.
Your Pardon for that Sir.

Sir Cred.
For look ye Sir, I'le tell you the Nature of Dogs and Horses.

Fat D.
So can my Groom and Dog-keeper, but what's this t'th' purpose Sir?

[Here they leave off.

Sir Cred.
To th' purpose Sir, good Mr. *Hedleburgh* do you understand what's to th' purpose? you're a *Dutch* Butter-ferkin, a Kilderkin, a Double Jugg.

Fat D.
You're an ignorant Blockhead Sir.

Sir Cred.
You lye Sir, and there I was with you again.

Amst.
What, quarrelling, men of your gravity and Profession!

Sir Cred.
That is to say Fools and Knaves, pray how long is't since you left Toping and Naping, for Quacking, good Brother Cater-tray,—but let that pass, for I'le have my Humour, and therefore will quarrell with no man, and so I drink.—

[Goes to fill again.

Brun.
—But what's all this to the Patient, Gentlemen?

Sir Cred.
Aye—the Wine's all out,—and quarrells apart Gentlemen as you say, what do ye think of our Patient, for something I conceive necessary to be said for our Fees.

Fat D.
I think that unless he follows our Prescriptions he's a dead man.

Sir Cred.
Aye Sir a dead man.

Fat D.
Please you to write Sir, you seem the youngest Doctor.

[To Amst.

Amst.
Your Pardon Sir, I conceive there may be younger Doctors then I at the board.

Sir Cred.
A fine Punctilio this, when a man lies a dying—Sir

> *[Aside.*

you shall excuse me, I have been a Doctor this 7 years.

> *[They shove the pen and paper from one to the other.*

Amst.
I Commenc't at *Paris* twenty years agoe.

Ley.
And I at *Leyden*, almost as long since.

Fat D.
And I at *Bercelona* thirty.

Sir Cred.
And I at *Padua*, Sir.

Fat D.
You at *Padua*?

Sir Cred.
Yes Sir I at *Padua*, why what a Pox do ye think I never was beyond-sea?

Brun.
However Sir you are the youngest Doctor and must write.

Sir Cred.
I will not lose an Inch of my Dignity.

Fat D.
Nor I.

Amst.
Nor I.

Ley.
Nor I.

Put the paper from each other

Brun.
Death what Rascalls are these?

Sir Cred.
Give me the pen—here's adoe about your *Paduas* and Punctilioes.

[Sets himself to write.

Amst.
Every Morning a Dose of my Pills *Merda quecrusticon,* or the Amicable Pill.

Sir Cred.
Fasting?

Ley.
Every hour Sixscore drops of *Adminicula Vitæ.*

Sir Cred.
—Fasting too?

[Sir Credulous writes still.

Sir Patient Fancy

Fat D.
At Night twelve Cordiall Pills, *Gallimofriticus*.

Turb.
Let bloud once a week, a Glister once a day.

Brun.
Cry Mercy Sir, you're a *French* man—After his first sleep, threescore restorative Pills call'd *Cheatus Redivivus*.

Sir Cred.
—And lastly, fifteen spoonfulls of my *Aqua Tetrachymagogon*, as often as 'tis necessary, little or no Breakfast, less Dinner, and go supperless to bed.

Fat D.
Hum, your *Aqua Tetrachymagogon*?

Sir Cred.
Yes Sir, my *Tetrachymagogon*, for look ye do ye see Sir, I cur'd the Arch-Duke of *Strumbulo*, of a *Gondileero*, of which he dy'd, with this very *Aqua Tetrachymagogon*.
Enter Sir Patient.

Sir Pat.
Well Gentlemen am I not an intruder?

Fat.
Sir we have duly consider'd the state of your Body: and are now about the order and method you are to observe.

Brun.
Aye this distemper will be the occasion of his death.

Sir Cred.
Hold Brothers, I do not say the occasion of his death: But the occasional cause of his death.

[Sir Pat. reads the Bill.

Sir Pat.
Why here's no time allow'd for eating Gentlemen.

Amst.
Sir we'le justify this Prescription to the whole College.

Ley.
If he will not follow it, let him dye.

All.
Aye let him dye.
Enter Lodwick and Leander.

Lod.
What have you consulted without me Gentlemen?

[Lod. reads the Bill.

Sir Pat.
Yes Sir, and find it absolutely necessary for my health Sir, I shou'd be starv'd: and yet you say I am not sick Sir.

[To Leand.

Lod.
Very well, very well.

Sir Pat.
No Breakfast, no Dinner, no Supper?

Sir Cred.
Little or none, but none's best.

Sir Pat.
But Gentlemen consider, no small thing?

All.
Nothing, nothing.

Sir Cred.
Sir, you must write for your Fee.

        [To Lod.

Lod.
Now I think on't Sir you may eat, *[writes]* a Rosted-Pippin cold upon a Vine leaf, at night.

Lean.
Do you see Sir, what damn'd canting Rascals these Doctors are?

Sir Pat.
Aye, aye, if all Doctors were such, ingeniously I shou'd soon be weary of Physick.

Lean.
Give 'em their Fees Sir, and send 'em to the Devil for a company of Cheats.

Sir Pat.
Truth is, there's no faith in 'em,—well I thank you for your care and pains.

        [gives 'em Fees.

Sir Cred.
Sir if you have any occasion for me, I live at the Red colour'd Lanthorn, with Eleven Candles in't, in the *Strand*; where you may come in privately, and need not be ashamed, I having no Creature in my House but my self, and my whole Family.—

[*Exeunt.*

Ick quam Van Neder Landt te spreken
End helpen Van Pocken end ander gebreken.
That's a top of my Bill sweet Sir.

Fan.
Lord, Sir Father, why did you give 'em money?

Lean.
For talking nonsense this hour or two upon his distemper.

Fan.
Oh lemini Sir, they did not talk one word of you, but of Dogs, and Horses, and of killing folks, and of their Wives and Daughters; and when the Wine was all out, they said they wou'd say something for their Fees.

Sir Pat.
Say you so?—Knaves, Rogues, Cheats, Murderers! I'le be reveng'd on 'em all,—I'le ne're be sick again,—or if I be I'le die honestly of my self without the assistance of such Rascals,—go, get you gone,—

[*To Fan. who goes out.*

Lean.
A happy resolution, wou'd you wou'd be so kind to your self as to make a trial of your Lady too, and if she prove true, 'twill make some kind of amends for your so long being couzen'd this way.

Sir Patient Fancy

Sir Pat.
I'le about it, this very minute about it,—give me a Chair.—

> [*He sits.*

Lean.
So, settle your self well, disorder your Hair,—throw away your Cane, Hat, and Gloves,—stare and rowl your eyes, squeez your Face into Convulsions,—clutch your hands,— make your Stomach heave,—so, very well,—now let me alone for the rest,—Oh, help, help my Lady, my Aunt, for Heavens sake help,—come all and see him die.

> [*Weeps.*

Enter Wittmore, Lady Fancy, Isabella, Lucretia, Lady Knowell, and Roger.

Witt.
Leander, what's the matter?

Lean.
See Madam, see my Uncle in the Agonies of Death.

La. Fa.
My dearest Husband dying, Oh!

> [*Weeps.*

Lean.
How hard he struggles with departing life!

Isab.
Father, dear Father, must I in one day receive a blessing with so great a curse? Oh,—he's just going Madam.—

> [*Weeps.*

Sir Patient Fancy

La. Fa.
Let me o'retake him in the shades below, why do you hold me, can I live without him?—do I dissemble well?—

[Aside to Witt.

Sir Pat.
Not live without me!—do you hear that sirrah?

[Aside to Lean.

Lean.
Pray Mark the end on't Sir,—feign,—feign,—

La. Kn.
We left him well, how came he thus o'th' suddain?

Lean.
I fear 'tis an Apoplexy Madam.

La. Fa.
Run, run for his Physician! but do not stir a foot.

[Aside to Roger.

Look up and speak but one kind word to me.

Sir Pat.
What cries are these that stop me on my way?

La. Fa.
They're mine,—your Ladies,—oh surely he'le recover, [Aside] your most obedient Wife's.

Sir Pat.
My Wife's my Heir, my sole Executrix.

La. Fa.
Hah, is he in's senses?*[Aside to Witt.]* Oh my dear Love, my Life, my Joy, my all, *[Cryes]* oh let me goe; I will not live without him.

        Seems to faint in Wittmore's Armes. All run about her.

Sir Pat.
Do ye hear that sirrah?

Lean.
Have yet a little patience, die away,—very well— Oh he's gone,—quite gone.

        La. Fa. swounds.

La. Kn.
Look to my Lady there, *[swounds again]*—sure she can but counterfeit. *[Aside.]*

        [They all go about her.

Sir Pat.
Hah, my Lady dying!

Lean.
Sir I beseech you wait the event; Death! the cunning Devil will dissemble too long and spoil all,—here—carry the dead Corps of my dearest Uncle to his Chamber. Nurse to your care I commit him now.

        [Exeunt with Sir Pat. in a Chair.

Sir Patient Fancy

All follow but Wittmore; who going the other way meets Sir Credulous and Lodwick, as before.

Witt.
Lodwick! the strangest unexpected News, Sir *Patient*'s Dead!

Sir Cred.
How, dead! we have play'd the Physicians to good purpose i'faith, and kill'd the man before we administred our Physick.

Witt.
Egad I fear so indeed.

Lod.
Dead!

Witt.
As a Herring, and 'twill be dangerous to keep these habits longer.

Sir Cred.
Dangerous! Zoz man we shall all be hang'd, why our very Bill dispatch'd him, and our Hands are to't,—oh, I'le confess all.—

[Offers to goe.

Lod.
Death Sir, I'le cut your Throat if you stir.

Sir Cred.
Wou'd you have me hang'd for company Gentlemen? Oh where shall I hide my self, or how come at my cloaths?

Sir Patient Fancy

Lod.
We have no time for that, go get you into your Basket again, and lie snug, till I have convey'd you safe away,—or I'le abandon you.— [*Aside to him.*] 'Tis not necessary he shou'd be seen yet, he may spoil *Leander*'s Plot.

[*Aside.*

Sir Cred.
Oh thank ye dear *Lodwick*,—let me escape this bout, and if ever the Fool turn Physician again, may he be choak'd with his own *Tetrachymagogon*.

Witt.
Go hast and undress you, whilst I'le to *Lucia*.

[*Ex. Lod.*
As Wittmore is going out at one Door, Enter Sir Patient and Leander at the other.

Lean.
Hah, *Wittmore* there! he must not see my Uncle yet.

[*Puts Sir Pat. back. Ex. Witt.*

Sir Pat.
Nay Sir, never detain me, I'le to my Lady, is this your Demonstration?—was ever so vertuous a Lady?— Well I'le to her, and console her poor heart, ah the joy 'twill bring her to see my Resurrection!—I long to surprize her.

[*Going off cross the Stage.*

Lean.
Hold Sir, I think she's coming,—blest sight, and with her *Wittmore*!

[*Puts Sir Pat. back to the door.*

Sir Patient Fancy

Enter Lady Fancy and Wittmore.

Sir Pat.
Hah, what's this?

La. Fa.
Now my dear *VVitmore*, claim thy Rites of Love without controll, without the contradiction of wretched Poverty or Jealousy: Now, undisguis'd thou maist approach my Bed, and reign o're all my Pleasures and my Fortunes, of which this minute I create thee Lord. And thus begin my Homage.—

[*Kisses him.*

Sir Pat.
Sure 'tis some Fiend! This cannot be my Lady!

Lean.
'Tis something uncivil before your face Sir, to do this.

VVitt.
Thou wondrous kind, and wondrous Beautiful, that Power that made thee with so many Charms, gave me a Soul fit onely to adore 'em; nor wert thou destin'd to another's Arms, but to be render'd still more fit for mine.

Sir Pat.
Hah, is not that *Fain-love*? *Isabella*'s Husband? Oh Villain! Villain! I will renounce my Sense and my Religion.

[*Aside.*

La. Fa.
Anothers Armes! Oh call not those hated thoughts to my remembrance,

Sir Patient Fancy

Lest it destroy that kindly heat within me,
Which thou canst onely raise, and still maintain.

Sir Pat.
Oh Woman! Woman! damn'd dissembling Woman!

> [*Aside.*

La. Fa.
Come let me lead thee to that Mass of Gold he gave me to be despis'd: And which I render thee, my lovely Conquerour, As the first Tribute of my Glorious Servitude,—Draw in the Basket which I told you of, and is amongst the Rubbish in the Hall, [*Ex. Wittmore.*] That which the Slave so many years was toiling for, I in one moment barter for a Kiss, as Earnest of our future Joys.

Sir Pat.
Was ever so prodigal a Harlot? was this the Saint? was this the most tender Consort that ever man had?

Lean.
No in good faith Sir.
Enter Wittmore pulling in the Basket.

La. Fa.
This is it with a direction on't to thee, whither I design'd to send it.

Witt.
Good morrow to the day, and next the Gold, open the Shrine, that I may see my Saint—hail the Worlds Soul—

> [*Opens the Basket, Sir Cred. starts up.*

La. Fa.
O Heavens! what thing art thou?

Sir Cred.
O Pardon, Pardon sweet Lady, I confess I had a hand in't.

La. Fa.
In what, thou slave?—

Sir Cred.
Killing the good believing Alderman,—but 'twas against my will.

La. Fa.
Then I'me not so much oblig'd to thee,—but where's the money, the 8000 *l.* the Plate and Jewels, sirrah?

VVitt.
Death the Dog has eat it.

Sir Cred.
Eat it! oh Lord, eat 8000 *l.* wou'd I might never come out of this Basket alive, if ever I made such a meal in my life.

VVitt.
Ye Dog you have eat it, and I'le make ye swallow all the Doses you writ in your Bill, but I'le have it upward or downward.

[*Aside.*

Sir Pat.
Hah, one of the Rogues my Doctours.

Sir Cred.
Oh dear Sir, hang me out of the way rather.
Enter Maundy.

Mau.
Madam, I have sent away the Basket to Mr. *VVittmores* Lodgings.

La. Fa.
You might have sav'd your self that labour, I now having no more to doe, but to bury the stinking Corps of my quondam Cuckold, dismiss his Daughters, and give thee quiet possession of all.

[To Witt.

Sir Pat.
Fair Lady, you'l take me along with you?

[Snaps.

[Pulls off his Hat and comes up to her.

La. Fa.
My Husband!—I'me betray'd—

Sir. Pat.
Husband! I do defie thee Satan, thou greater Whore than she of *Babylon*: thou shame, thou abomination to thy Sex.

La. Fa.
Rail on, whilst I dispose my self to laugh at thee.

Sir Pat.
Leander, call all the House in, to be a witness of our Divorce.

[Ex. Leander.

La. Fa.
Do, and all the World, and let 'em know the Reason.

Sir Pat.

Sir Patient Fancy

Methinks I find an inclination to swear,—to curse my self and thee, that I cou'd no better discern thee; nay, I'me so chang'd from what I was, that I think I cou'd even approve of Monarchy and Church Discipline, I'me so truly convinc'd I have been a beast and an ass all my life.

Enter La. Know. Isabella, Lucre. Lean. Lodwick, Fan. &c.

La. Kn.
Hah, Sir *Patient* not dead?

Sir Pat.
Ladies and Gentlemen, take notice that I am Cuckold, a Crop-ear'd snivelling Cuckold.

Sir Cred.
A Cuckold! sweet Sir, shaw that's a small matter in a man of your Quality.

Sir Pat.
And I beg your pardon Madam, for being angry that you call'd me so. *[To La. Know.]* And yours, Dear *Isabella*, for desiring you to marry my good Friend there *[points to Witt.]* whose Name I perceive I was mistaken in:—And yours *Leander*, that I wou'd not take your Advice long since: And yours fair Lady, for believing you honest,—twas done like a credulous Coxcomb:—And yours Sir, for taking any of your Tribe for Wise, Learn'd, or Honest.

[To Sir Credulous.

Witt.
Faith Sir, I deceiv'd ye onely to serve my Friend, and Sir, your Daughter is married to Mr. *Knowell*; your Wife had all my stock of Love before, Sir.

[Lod. and Isab. kneel.

Sir Pat.
Why God-a-mercy—some comfort that,—God bless ye—I shall love disobedience while I live for't.

Lod.
I'me glad on't Sir, for then I hope you will forgive *Leander*, who has married my Sister and not my Mother.

Sir Pat.
How! has he serv'd me so,—I'le make him my Heir for't; thou hast made a Man of me my Boy, and faith we will be merry,—fair Lady, you may depart in peace fair Lady, restoring my Money, my Plate, my Jewels and my Writings, fair Lady—.

La. Fa.
You gave me no Money Sir, prove it if you can, and for your Land, 'twas not settled with this Proviso, If she be Honest?

Sir Pat.
'Tis well thou dost confess I am a Cuckold, for I wou'd have it known, fair Lady.

La. Fa.
'Twas to that End I married you, good Alderman.

Sir Pat.
I'faith I think thou didst sweet-heart, I'faith I think thou didst.

VVitt.
Right Sir, for we have long been Lovers, but want of Fortune made us contrive how to marry her to your good Worship. Many a wealthy Citizen Sir, has contributed to the maintenance of a younger Brother's Mistress, and you are not the first Man in Office that has been a Cuckold, Sir.

Sir Patient Fancy

Sir Pat.
Some comfort that too, the Brethren of the Chain cannot laugh at me.

Sir Cred.
A very pleasant old Fellow this faith, I cou'd be very merry with him now but that I am damnable sad, — Madam, I shall desire to lay the Saddle on the right Horse.

[*To La. Know.*

La. Kn.
What mean you Sir?

Sir Cred.
Onely Madam, if I were as some men are, I should not be as I am.

La. Kn.
It may be so Sir.

Sir Cred.
I say no more, but matters are not carry'd so swimmingly, but I can dive into the meaning on't.

[*Sir Patient talks this while to Lodw.*

La. Kn.
I hate this Hypothetical way of arguing, answer me Categorically.

Sir Cred.
Hypothetical and Categorical! what does she mean now? [*Aside.*] — Madam, in plain English I am made a *John A-Nokes* of, *Jack-hold-my-staff*, a *Merry Andrew* Doctor to give *Leander* time to marry your Daughter, and 'twas therefore I was hoisted up in the Basket, — but as the Play says, 'tis well 'tis no worse: I'de rather lose my Mistress then my life.

Sir Patient Fancy

Sir Pat.
But how came this Rascal *Turboon* to admit you?

Lod.
For the lucre of our fees Sir, which was his recompence.

Sir Pat.
I forgive it you, and will turn Spark, they live the merriest lives— keep some City Mistress, go to Court, and hate all Conventicles.

You see what a fine City Wife can doe
Of the true breed: Instruct her Husband too:
I wish all civil Cuckolds in the Nation,
Would take Example by my Reformation.

Lightning Source UK Ltd.
Milton Keynes UK
UKOW051806140312

188987UK00001B/31/P